Drunk Driving Laws

Rules of the Road When Crossing State Lines

Attorney
Dennis A. Bjorklund

PRAETORIAN PUBLISHERS

This publication is merely the commencement of dialogue with the readers, and we welcome suggestions to update the book for reprint and future editions. Send all comments to the address hereinbelow.

Library of Congress Catalog Card Number: 98-68103

Bjorklund, Dennis A.
Drunk Driving Laws: Rules of the Road When Crossing State Lines.

1. Drunk Driving--United States. 2. Defense (Criminal procedure)--United States. I. Title.

First published in the United States of America in 1997
ISBN: 1-57502-987-1

PRAETORIAN PUBLISHERS
P.O. Box 1847, Iowa City, Iowa 52240-1847
Morris Publishing
3212 E. Hwy 30
Kearney, NE 68847
1-800-650-7888

CONTENTS

AUTHOR BIOGRAPHY

Dennis A. Bjorklund is an attorney specializing in drunk driving defense. He has written the only authoritative drunk driving books aimed at helping motorists protect their legal and constitutional rights against the unlawful infringement of law enforcement officers.

Drunk Driving Defense: How to Beat the Rap is a comprehensive synopsis at every phase of a drunk driving case, from the initial police stop through trial, with powerful insight into secret tactics used by law enforcement officers and prosecutors, and effective ways to avoid a conviction.

Drunk Driving: A Survival Guide for Motorists is a summary of the constitutional and statutory rights of motorists involved in a drunk driving case, including a thorough review of the drunk driving laws, criminal penalties, driver's license sanctions, and practical suggestions to avoid future legal problems.

Drunk Driving Laws: Rules of the Road When Crossing State Lines is a state by state overview of drunk driving laws, encompassing the legal standard for a criminal charge, penalties, driver's license sanctions, implied consent procedures, and chemical testing requirements.

Additional drunk driving-related books that were written specifically for motorists are scheduled for future release. *Drunk Driving and the Driver's License Suspension: How to Get Back on the Road* is intended to simplify the department of transportation bureaucracy so motorists can understand the administrative requirements and procedural aspects necessary to obtain a temporary restricted license (work permit), to calculate suspension periods, and achieve license reinstatement.

The Author has an extensive résumé of scholarly accomplishments, which include writing for the Iowa Law Review and being hand-selected as a distinguished literary contributor to author articles within his area of specialty.

Introduction

In recent years drunk driving offenses have become one of the most publicized and legislatively active areas. During each session at least one state congressional representative introduces legislation to increase the penalties associated with this activity. More often than not, the proposed changes become law, so it is very difficult for motorists to stay abreast of the legal requirements (and penalties) for a drunk driving charge.

The purpose of this book is to provide motorists with crucial information that is necessary to understand each state's drunk driving laws. Relevant statutory provisions allow interested readers to thoroughly research specific aspects of this crime and vital legal terms are provided, such as the definition of driving and legal impairment. There are also sections on the legal requirements for a drunk driving charge, criminal punishment, and the penalty enhancement period used to calculate multiple offenses.

Additionally, motorists are given specific information on implied consent laws, the legal obligation of police officers to advise defendants of their rights, various driver's license sanctions, and the right to an independent chemical test. The text also includes the statutory requirements for chemical testing, information on the governmental body that regulates the procedures, and the defendant's right to know the test results. Finally, if applicable, a section is devoted to the defendant's statutory right to have a drunk driving charge reduced or dismissed.

Although every attempt was made to include the most current laws, the statutory provisions are subject to change with each legislative session so use the book as a general guide. If you are searching for precise information, consult a lawyer specializing in drunk driving defense or personally research the statutory provisions. Each state has innumerable laws dealing with minor details of a drunk driving charge. These details were omitted to remain true to the primary goal of the book: to provide motorists with a quick and easy reference that contains the most vital information on drunk driving laws.

State laws usually have more severe penalties for drunk driving incidents that involve children in the vehicle, excessive speed, property damage, serious personal injury, or death. There may be sentencing options available in lieu of minimum jail sentences, such as deferred judgments, suspended sentences, probation or diversion programs.

Furthermore, the driver's license sanction often provides a range of suspension periods that encompass a multitude of circumstances, such as refusing or consenting to a chemical test. As the number of drunk driving offenses increases, there is a steady increase in the severity of the driver's license suspension. For example, if the suspension range is six months to ten years, the first offense would be six months, the second offense may be one year, the third offense three years, and the fourth offense ten years.

In some instances, minimum statutory fines can be waived or substituted for community service. Other times there will be additional expenses associated with a conviction, such as a surcharge, assessment fee, highway fund expense, driver's license reinstatement fee, substance abuse evaluation and treatment charge, or court costs.

Finally, there could be additional requirements, like drunk driving classes, counseling, intensive substance abuse treatment, or reality-based education sessions. In other words, do not solely rely on this book to specify every detail of the punishment or costs involved with a drunk driving offense; the law may change and there may be options available that only a lawyer can answer.

ALABAMA

Relevant Statute: §§ 32-5A-191 to 32-5A-194

Definition of Driving: Driving or actual physical control of a vehicle.

Drunk Driving Offenses:
(1) BAC of .08 or more.
(2) Under the influence of alcohol, controlled substance, or any combination thereof.
(3) Under the influence of any substance that impairs the driver's mental or physical faculties.

Legal Impairment:
(1) Alcohol offense: Any degree of impairment.
(2) Other offenses: Incapable of safely driving.

Penalty Enhancement: 5 years

Penalties:
(1) First offense: Maximum 1 year in jail; $600-$2,000 fine; 90-day license suspension.
(2) Second offense: Maximum 1 year in jail (minimum 48 consecutive hours or 20 days of community service); $1,100-$5,100 fine; 1-year license revocation.
(3) Third offense: 60 days to 1 year in jail; $2,100-$10,100 fine; 3-year license revocation.
(4) Fourth or subsequent offense (class C felony): 1-10 years in prison, $4,100-$10,100 fine; 5-year license revocation.

Implied Consent Laws:
(1) Chemical Tests Allowed: Breath or urine as selected by officer; blood test with driver's consent.
(2) Advisement Required: License suspension for test refusal.

(3) Test Refusal: 90-day or 1-year license suspension; admissible in any proceeding arising out of same incident.
(4) Test Result: No immediate license sanction.

Chemical Testing:
(1) Legal Aspects: All chemical tests must be performed by a person with a valid permit in accordance with methods approved by Department of Forensic Sciences; court may take judicial notice of departmental methods.
(2) Blood Test: Withdrawal for police testing must be administered by a physician, registered nurse, or other qualified person.
(3) Test Result: Upon written request, results must be provided to the defendant.
(4) Independent Chemical Test: In addition to any police test, defendants have the right to request and pay for an independent chemical test from a qualified person of their choice. The failure or inability to obtain an additional test does not preclude the admissibility of the police test.

ALASKA

Relevant Statute: §§ 28.15.181; 28.35.029 to 28.40

Definition of Driving: Operating, driving or having actual physical control of a motor vehicle, aircraft or watercraft.

Drunk Driving Offenses:
(1) BAC of .10 or more within 4 hours of driving.
(2) Under the influence of intoxicating liquor, controlled substance, or any combination thereof.

Legal Impairment: None specified.

Penalty Enhancement: 5 and 10 years

Penalties:

(1) First offense: 72 hours to 1 year in jail; minimum $250 fine; 90-day license revocation.

(2) Second offense: 20 days to 1 year in jail; minimum $500 fine; minimum 1-year license revocation; vehicle forfeiture.

(3) Third offense:
Within 5 years: Minimum 120 days in jail; minimum $5,000 fine; minimum 3-year license revocation; vehicle forfeiture.
Within 10 years: 60 days to 1 year in jail; minimum $1,000 fine; minimum 3-year license revocation; vehicle forfeiture.

(4) Fourth offense:
Within 5 years: Minimum 240 days in jail; minimum $5,000 fine; minimum 3-year license revocation; vehicle forfeiture.
Within 10 years: 120 days in jail; minimum $2,000 fine; minimum 5-year license revocation; vehicle forfeiture.

(5) Fifth offense:
Within 5 years: Minimum 360 days in jail; minimum $5,000 fine; minimum 3-year license revocation; vehicle forfeiture.
Within 10 years: 240 days in jail; minimum $3,000 fine; minimum 5-year license revocation; vehicle forfeiture.

(6) Sixth offense:
Within 5 years: 360 days in jail; minimum $4,000 fine; permanent license revocation; vehicle forfeiture.
Within 10 years: 240 days in jail; minimum $3,000 fine; minimum 5-year license revocation; vehicle forfeiture.

Implied Consent Laws:

(1) Chemical Tests Allowed: Blood or breath for alcohol; blood or urine for drugs; PBT.

(2) Advisement Required: Penalties for refusal; refusal is an infraction; admissible in civil and criminal proceedings.

(3) Test Refusal (class A misdemeanor): Admissible in any proceeding arising out of same incident; PBT refusal is an infraction.

(4) Test Result: BAC .10 or more: 90-day to 5-year license revocation.

Chemical Testing:

(1) Legal Aspects: Chemical test is presumed valid if performed in accordance with methods approved by Department of Public Safety within 4 hours of driving.

(2) Blood Test: Withdrawal for police testing must be administered by a physician, qualified technician, chemist, registered nurse, or other qualified person.

(3) Test Result: Upon written request, results must be provided to the defendant.

(4) Independent Chemical Test: In addition to any police test, defendants have the right to request and pay for an independent chemical test from a qualified person of their choice. The failure or inability to obtain an additional test does not preclude the admissibility of the police test. An unsuccessful attempt at independent testing is admissible evidence.

ARIZONA

Relevant Statute: §§ 28-691 to 28-696

Definition of Driving: Driving or actual physical control of any vehicle within the state.

Drunk Driving Offenses:

(1) BAC of .10 or more (.04 for commercial vehicles) within 2 hours of driving.

(2) Under the influence of intoxicating liquor, any drug, or vapor releasing substance containing a toxic substance, or any combination thereof.

(3) Driving with any drug or its metabolite in the person's body.

Legal Impairment: To the slightest degree.

Penalty Enhancement: 5 years

Penalties:

(1) First offense: 10 days to 6 months in jail (minimum 24 hours with substance abuse class); maximum 40 hours of community service; $250-$2,000 fine; 90-day license suspension.

(2) Second offense: 90 days to 6 months in jail (minimum 30 days with substance abuse class); $500-$2,000 fine; 1-year license revocation.

(3) Third or subsequent offense (class 5 felony): 8 months to 1½ years in prison; maximum $150,000 fine; 3-year license revocation.

Implied Consent Laws:

(1) Chemical Tests Allowed: Blood, breath or urine as selected by officer.

(2) Advisement Required: License suspension periods.

(3) Test Refusal: Immediate license seizure; 12-month license suspension; admissible in any proceeding arising out of same incident.

(4) Test Result: BAC .10 or more: minimum 90-day license suspension.

Chemical Testing:

(1) Legal Aspects: Breath test results are admissible if performed by a person with a valid permit in accordance to an operational checklist for instruments approved and maintained by the Department of Health Service, and duplicate tests are administered with results within .02 of each other (or the defendant was observed for 20 minutes immediately prior to the test).

(2) Blood Test: Withdrawal for police testing must be administered by a physician, registered nurse, or other qualified person, other than the arresting officer.

(3) Test Result: No statutory provision for disclosure.

(4) Independent Chemical Test: In addition to any police test, defendants must be given a reasonable opportunity to arrange and pay for an independent chemical test from a qualified person of their choice. The failure or inability to obtain an additional test does not preclude the admissibility of the police test.

Plea Agreements: If a DUI or per se offense lacks sufficient legal or factual basis, it can be dismissed or reduced to a misdemeanor or petty offense.

ARKANSAS

Relevant Statute: §§ 5-65-102 to 5-65-207

Definition of Driving: Operating or actual physical control of a motor vehicle.

Drunk Driving Offenses:
(1) BAC of .10 or more.
(2) Under the influence of alcohol, a controlled substance, any intoxicant, or any combination thereof.

Legal Impairment: Reactions, motor skills, and judgment are substantially altered.

Penalty Enhancement: 3 years

Penalties:
(1) First offense: 24 hours to 1 year in jail; $150-$1,000 fine; 90 to 120-day license suspension.
(2) Second offense: 7 days to 1 year in jail; $400-$3,000 fine; 1-year to 16-month license suspension.
(3) Third offense: 90 days to 1 year in jail; $900-$5,000 fine; 2-year to 30-month license suspension.
(4) Fourth or subsequent offense (a felony): 1-6 years in prison; $900-$5,000 fine; 4-year license suspension; vehicle forfeiture.

Implied Consent Laws:
(1) Chemical Tests Allowed: Blood, breath or urine as selected by officer; blood test requires consent.
(2) Advisement Required: Right to independent test.

(3) Test Refusal: Immediate license seizure; 180-day to lifetime license suspension; admissible in all proceedings arising out of same incident.
(4) Test Result: Immediate license seizure.

Chemical Testing:
(1) Legal Aspects: Chemical tests must be performed by a person with a valid permit in accordance with approved methods and certified equipment that complies with rules and regulations adopted by the State Board of Health and the State Department of Health.
(2) Blood Test: No statutory provision authorizing specific individuals to perform the test.
(3) Test Result: Upon written request, results must be provided to the defendant.
(4) Independent Chemical Test: In addition to any police test, defendants must be given a reasonable opportunity to arrange and pay for an independent chemical test from a qualified person of their choice. If the officer does not advise of this right, or fails to permit or assist the defendant in obtaining a test, the police test is inadmissible.

Plea Agreements: Drunk driving offenses cannot be reduced.

CALIFORNIA

Relevant Statute: §§ 23152 to 23176; 23195; also 23212; 13353

Definition of Driving: Driving or actual physical control of a vehicle.

Drunk Driving Offenses:
(1) BAC of .08 or more (.04 for commercial vehicles).
(2) Under the influence of an alcoholic beverage, any drug, or combination thereof.
(3) Driving by a person addicted to any drug, except persons in a narcotic treatment program.

Legal Impairment: To an appreciable degree.

Penalty Enhancement: 7 years

Penalties:

(1) First offense: 96 hours to 6 months in jail; $390-$1,000 fine; 90-day to 6-month license suspension.
(2) Second offense: 90 days to 1 year in jail; $390-$1,000 fine; 12 to 18-month license suspension; vehicle impoundment.
(3) Third offense: 120 days to 1 year in jail; $390-$1,000 fine; license revocation; vehicle impoundment and forfeiture.
(4) Fourth or subsequent offense: 180 days to 1 year in jail; $390-$1,000 fine; license revocation; vehicle impoundment and forfeiture.

Implied Consent Laws:

(1) Chemical Tests Allowed: Defendant selects the test; blood, breath or urine for alcohol; blood or urine for drugs; PBT.
(2) Advisement Required: Criminal punishment and fine; driver's license suspension periods; choice of tests; penalties for refusal; refusal is admissible in court; no right to have attorney present; breath sample will not be preserved; blood or urine sample will be preserved for later testing.
(3) Test Refusal: 1 to 3-year license suspension and enhancement of charged offense; admissible evidence; right to refuse PBT.
(4) Test Result: BAC .08 or more: 4-month to 1-year license suspension.

Chemical Testing:

(1) Legal Aspects: Standards for withdrawing, handling and preserving blood samples are adopted by the State Department of Human Services.
(2) Blood Test: Withdrawal for police testing must be administered by a licensed physician and surgeon, registered nurse, licensed vocational nurse, duly licensed clinical laboratory technologist or bioanalyst, unlicensed but regulated laboratory personnel, or certified paramedic.
(3) Test Result: Upon request, results must be given to the defendant.

(4) Independent Chemical Test: In addition to any police test, defendants must be given a reasonable opportunity to arrange and pay for an independent chemical test from a qualified person of their choice. The failure or inability to obtain an additional test does not preclude the admissibility of the police test.

Plea Agreements: When the prosecution dismisses, substitutes or reduces a § 23152 offense, or when an enhancement offense is reduced, written reasons must be made part of the court record. If a § 23152 offense is reduced to reckless driving (CVC §§ 23103), certain reporting and disclosure provisions apply.

COLORADO

Relevant Statute: §§ 42-4-1301; also 42-1-102 and 42-2-122

Definition of Driving: Driving or actual physical control of any vehicle upon the streets, highways, and throughout the state.

Drunk Driving Offenses:
(1) BAC of .10 or more for blood or breath within 2 hours of driving. (per se offense)
(2) Under the influence of alcohol, drugs, or combination thereof. (DUI offense)
(3) Impaired by alcohol, drugs, or combination thereof. (impaired offense)
(4) Driving by habitual users of any controlled substance.

Legal Impairment:
(1) DUI offense: Substantially incapable, either mentally or physically, to exercise clear judgment, sufficient physical control, or due care in the safe operation of a vehicle.
(2) Impaired offense: To the slightest degree, the defendant is less able than ordinary, either mentally or physically, to exercise clear judgment, sufficient physical control, or due care in the safe operation of a vehicle.

Penalty Enhancement: 5 years

Penalties:
(1) First DUI or per se offense: 5 days to 1 year in jail; 48-96 hours of public service; $300-$1,000 fine.
(2) Second or subsequent DUI or per se offense: 90 days to 1 year in jail; 60-120 hours of public service; $500-$1,500 fine.
(3) First DUI or per se conviction with prior impaired conviction: 70 days to 1 year in jail; 56-112 hours of public service; $450-$1,500 fine.
(4) First impaired conviction: 2-180 days in jail; 24-48 hours of public service; $100-$500 fine.
(5) Second impaired conviction: 45 days to 1 year in jail; 48-96 hours of public service; $300-$1,000 fine.
(6) Impaired conviction with prior DUI or per se conviction: 60 days to 1 year in jail; 52-104 hours of public service; $400-$1,200 fine.

Implied Consent Laws:
(1) Chemical Tests Allowed: Officer selects test; blood or breath for alcohol; blood, urine or saliva for drugs; PBT.
(2) Advisement Required: None.
(3) Test Refusal: 1-year license revocation; no penalty for refusing PBT; admissible in criminal case.
(4) Test Result: BAC .10 or more: 3-month license revocation.

Chemical Testing:
(1) Legal Aspects: Chemical tests for police testing must be administered in accordance with the rules and regulations of the Department of Health. Strict compliance with regulations is not required.
(2) Blood Test: Withdrawal for police testing must be administered by a physician, registered nurse, certified paramedic, emergency medical technician or person whose normal duties include withdrawing blood under the supervision of a physician or registered nurse.
(3) Test Result: No statutory provision for disclosure.
(4) Independent Chemical Test: No statutory provision.

Plea Agreements: If the prosecuting attorney notifies the court that a prima facie case could not be established to substantiate the charge, an alcohol or drug related traffic offense can be reduced to a non-alcohol or non-drug related traffic offense.

CONNECTICUT

Relevant Statute: § 14-227

Definition of Driving: Operating a motor vehicle on a public road, private road with a statutory speed limit, parking area for ten or more cars, or any school property. Driving includes operating, steering or directing the course of a motor vehicle being towed by another motor vehicle.

Drunk Driving Offenses:
(1) BAC of .10 or more. (per se offense)
(2) Under the influence of intoxicating liquor, any drug, or combination thereof. (DUI offense)
(3) Ability impaired by the consumption of intoxicating liquor. (impaired offense)

Legal Impairment: Ability to function properly is diminished to an appreciable degree. BAC of .071 to .099 is deemed impaired.

Penalty Enhancement: 10 years

Penalties:
(1) First DUI or per se offense: 48 hours to 6 months in jail; 100 hours of community service; $500-$1,000 fine; 1-year license suspension.
(2) Second DUI or per se offense: 10 days to 1 year in jail; $500-$2,000 fine; 2-year license suspension.
(3) Third DUI or per se offense: 120 days to 2 years in jail; $1,000-$4,000 fine; 3-year license suspension.

(4) Fourth or subsequent DUI or per se offense: 1-3 years in prison; $2,000-$8,000 fine; permanent license revocation.
(5) Impaired driving offense (infraction): $35-$90 fine.

Implied Consent Laws:
(1) Chemical Tests Allowed: Blood, breath or urine as selected by officer. Blood test requires consent.
(2) Advisement Required: Constitutional rights; penalties for refusal; refusal is admissible evidence; reasonable opportunity to contact attorney.
(3) Test Refusal: Immediate license seizure; 1 to 2-year license suspension. Admissible in criminal case.
(4) Test Result: BAC .10 or more: 90-day to 18-month license suspension.

Chemical Testing:
(1) Legal Aspects: Chemical test results are admissible if the defendant consented to the test after being allowed to contact an attorney; was notified of results; test was checked for accuracy and performed by a certified person using methods and equipment approved by the Department of Public Health; a second identical chemical test was performed or reasonably attempted; test taken within 2 hours of the alleged offense. In DUI cases, chemical test results are only admissible at the defendant's request.
(2) Blood Test: Withdrawal for police testing must be administered by a licensed physician or surgeon, phlebotomist, qualified laboratory technician, emergency medical technician II, or registered nurse.
(3) Test Result: Must be mailed or delivered to the defendant within one business day after results are known.
(4) Independent Chemical Test: No statutory provision.

Plea Agreements: If the prosecuting attorney provides the court with specific reasons, a DUI or per se offense may be reduced or dismissed.

DELAWARE

Relevant Statute: 21 §§ 4177A-B; 21 §§ 2745 to 2750; also 11 § 3505

Definition of Driving: Driving, operating or having actual physical control of a vehicle, off-highway vehicle, or moped.

Drunk Driving Offenses:
(1) BAC of .10 or more within 4 hours of the alleged offense. (per se offense)
(2) Under the influence of alcohol, any drug, or combination thereof. (DUI offense)

Legal Impairment: None specified.

Penalty Enhancement: 5 years

Penalties:
(1) First offense: 60 days to 6 months in jail; $230-$1,150 fine; 1-year license revocation.
(2) Second or subsequent offense: 60 days to 18 months in jail; $575-$2,300 fine; 1-year license revocation.
(3) Third offense (class G felony): 1-2 years in prison; $1,000-$3,000 fine; 18-month license revocation.
(4) Fourth or subsequent offense (class E felony): 2-5 years in prison; $2,000-$6,000 fine; 18-month license revocation.

Implied Consent Laws:
(1) Chemical Tests Allowed: Officer selects test; blood, breath or urine for alcohol; blood or urine for drugs; PBT.
(2) Advisement Required: Implied consent penalties for refusal.
(3) Test Refusal: 1 to 2-year license revocation; no penalty for refusing PBT; admissible at trial.
(4) Test Result: BAC .10 or more: 3 to 18-month license suspension.

Chemical Testing:
(1) Legal Aspects: All chemical tests must be performed by a person with a valid permit in accordance with an approved facility using reliable procedures; no doctor-patient privilege.
(2) Blood Test: Withdrawal for police testing must be administered by a licensed physician, registered nurse, licensed practical nurse, or other properly trained individual.
(3) Test Result: Must be made available when defendant pleads not guilty.
(4) Independent Chemical Test: No statutory provision.

Plea Agreements: First offense charges can be dismissed if: (1) no prior DUI convictions; (2) fewer than 3 moving violations within last 2 years; (3) not involved in a personal injury accident; (4) BAC less than .20; (5) a valid license at the time of the offense; (6) complete any court-ordered probation for further instruction or rehabilitation. A probation violation results in a conviction, first-offense punishment.

DISTRICT OF COLUMBIA

Relevant Statute: §§ 40-505 to 40-507; 40-716 to 40-717

Definition of Driving: Operating or in physical control of any vehicle in the District.

Drunk Driving Offenses:
(1) BAC of .10 or more. (per se offense)
(2) Under the influence of intoxicating liquor, any drug, or combination thereof. (OWI offense)
(3) Ability impaired by consumption of intoxicating liquor. (impaired offense)

Legal Impairment: None specified.

Penalty Enhancement: 15 years

Penalties:

(1) First offense (OWI or per se offense): Maximum 90 days in jail; $300 fine; license revocation.

(2) Second offense (OWI or per se offense): Maximum 1 year in jail; $1,000-$5,000 fine; license revocation.

(3) Third or subsequent offense (OWI or per se offense): Maximum 1 year in jail; $2,000-$10,000 fine; license revocation.

(4) First offense (impaired offense): Maximum 30 days in jail; $200-$300 fine; license revocation.

(5) Second offense (impaired offense): Maximum 90 days in jail; $300-$500 fine; license revocation.

(6) Third or subsequent offense (impaired offense): Maximum 1 year in jail; $1,000-$5,000 fine; license revocation.

Implied Consent Laws:

(1) Chemical Tests Allowed: Blood, breath or urine as selected by arresting officer; PBT.

(2) Advisement Required: Penalties for refusal; right to request testimony of person administering test.

(3) Test Refusal: 12-month license revocation; admissible in any proceeding arising out of the same incident.

(4) Test Result: No immediate license sanction.

Chemical Testing:

(1) Legal Aspects: Chemical test result admissible without testimony if administered in accordance with manufacturer specifications and equipment tested for accuracy within the past 3 months (or the chief toxicologist certifies the test is accurate). Defendant can compel the officer or technician to testify regarding the accuracy of the test result; failure to request testimony is a waiver of this right. The Mayor is authorized to issue rules regarding the implied consent and chemical testing laws.

(2) Blood Test: Withdrawal for police testing must be administered by a physician or registered nurse.

(3) Test Result: Must be provided to the defendant.

(4) Independent Chemical Test: In addition to any police test, defendants have the right to request and pay for an independent chemical test from a qualified person of their choice. The

failure or inability to obtain an additional test does not preclude the admissibility of the police test.

FLORIDA

Relevant Statute: §§ 316.193; also 316.1932 to 316.1934

Definition of Driving: Driving or in actual physical control of a vehicle within the state.

Drunk Driving Offenses:
(1) BAC of .08 or more.
(2) Under the influence of alcohol, a chemical substance, or a controlled substance.

Legal Impairment: To the extent that normal faculties are impaired.

Penalty Enhancement: 5 years; 10 years for third or subsequent offenses.

Penalties:
(1) First offense:
BAC below .20: Maximum 6 months in jail; $250-$500 fine; 6-month license suspension.
BAC .20 or more: Maximum 9 months in jail; $500-$1,000 fine; 6-month license suspension.
(2) Second offense:
BAC below .20: 10 days to 9 months in jail; $500-$1,000 fine; 1-year license suspension.
BAC .20 or more: Maximum 12 months in jail; $1,000-$2,000 fine; vehicle impoundment; 1-year license suspension.
(3) Third offense:
BAC below .20: Maximum 12 months in jail; $1,000-$2,500 fine; 1-year license suspension.
BAC .20 or more: 30 days to 12 months in jail; $2,000-$5,000 fine; vehicle impoundment; 1-year license suspension.

(4) Fourth or subsequent offense (3rd degree felony): 30 days to 5 years in prison; $1,000-$5,000 fine; 1-year license suspension; vehicle impoundment.

Implied Consent Laws:

(1) Chemical Tests Allowed: Blood, breath and urine; urine for drugs; blood when accident involves serious personal injury or death; PBT.

(2) Advisement Required: Penalties for test refusal.

(3) Test Refusal: 1-year to 18-month license suspension; admissible in criminal proceeding.

(4) Test Result: BAC .08 or more: 6-month license suspension.

Chemical Testing:

(1) Legal Aspects: Chemical tests are presumed valid if performed by a person with a valid permit in accordance with an approved facility using reliable procedures, and the officer certifies substantial compliance with rules and regulations adopted by the Department of Law Enforcement.

(2) Blood Test: Withdrawal for police testing must be administered by a physician, certified paramedic, registered nurse, licensed practical nurse, or other authorized hospital personnel.

(3) Test Result: Upon request, results must be provided to the defendant.

(4) Independent Chemical Test: In addition to any police test, or if one is not requested by the officer, defendants have the right to request and pay for an independent chemical test from a qualified person of their choice. The officer must assist the defendant in procuring a test. The failure or inability to obtain an additional test does not preclude the admissibility of the police test.

Plea Agreements: When the BAC is .20 or more, or the charge involves certain aggravated drunk driving offenses, the court can refuse to accept a guilty plea to a lesser charge.

GEORGIA

Relevant Statute: §§ 40-6-391 to 40-6-392; 40-5-55 to 40-5-67

Definition of Driving: Driving or actual physical control of a moving vehicle upon the highways or throughout the state.

Drunk Driving Offenses:
(1) BAC of .10 or more (.04 for commercial vehicles or minors) within 3 hours of driving.
(2) Under the influence of alcohol, marijuana, drugs, a controlled substance, or combination thereof.

Legal Impairment: To the extent that it is less safe to drive.

Penalty Enhancement: 5 years

Penalties:
(1) First offense: 10 days to 12 months in jail (minimum 24 hours in jail and 20 hours of community service); $300-$1,000 fine; 1-year license suspension.
(2) Second offense: 90 days to 12 months in jail (minimum 48 hours in jail and 40-80 hours of community service); $600-$1,000 fine; 3-year license suspension.
(3) Third or subsequent offense (habitual violator): 120 days to 12 months in jail (minimum 10 days in jail and 40 hours of community service); $1,000-$5,000 fine; 5-year license revocation; vehicle forfeiture; publication of defendant's name and photograph.

Implied Consent Laws:
(1) Chemical Tests Allowed: Blood, breath or urine as selected by officer.
(2) Advisement Required: Penalties for consent or refusal of test; refusal is admissible evidence in all proceedings; license suspension periods; right to independent test.
(3) Test Refusal: Minimum 1-year license suspension; admissible in any criminal trial.

(4) Test Result: BAC .10 or more: minimum 1-year license suspension.

Chemical Testing:

(1) Legal Aspects: Blood, breath or urine test must be performed by a person with a valid permit in accordance to approved methods and certified equipment that complies with rules and regulations adopted by the Division of Forensic Sciences of the Georgia Bureau of Investigation. Duplicate tests are administered with results within .02 of each other.

(2) Blood Test: Withdrawal for police testing must be administered by a physician, registered nurse, laboratory technician, emergency medical technician, or other qualified person.

(3) Test Result: Upon request, results must be provided to the defendant.

(4) Independent Chemical Test: In addition to any police test, defendants have the right to request and pay for an independent chemical test from a qualified person of their choice. The failure or inability to obtain an additional test does not preclude the admissibility of the police test.

Plea Agreements: No statutory provision; special requirements for plea of no contest.

HAWAII

Relevant Statute: §§ 291-4 to 291-7; 286-151 to 286-153

Definition of Driving: Driving or assuming actual physical control of a motor vehicle or moped upon the public highways.

Drunk Driving Offenses:

(1) BAC of .08 or more. (per se offense)

(2) Under the influence of intoxicating liquor or any drug. (OWI offense)

Legal Impairment:

(1) OWI drugs: Diminished ability to operate a vehicle in careful and prudent manner.

(2) OWI intoxicating liquor: Sufficient impairment of normal mental faculties or ability to care for oneself and guard against casualty.

Penalty Enhancement: 5 years

Penalties:

(1) First offense: 48 hours to 5 days in jail; 72 hours of community service; $150-$1,000 fine; 90-day license suspension.

(2) Second offense: 48 hours to 14 days in jail; 100 hours of community service (80 hours for OWI drugs offense); $500-$1,500 fine; 1-year license suspension.

(3) Third offense: 10-30 days in jail; $500-$2,500 fine; 1 to 5-year license revocation.

(4) Third offense (OWI drugs): 10-180 days in jail; $500-$1,000 fine; 1 to 5-year license revocation.

Implied Consent Laws:

(1) Chemical Tests Allowed: Blood or breath as selected by officer.

(2) Advisement Required: Penalties for refusal.

(3) Test Refusal: 1 to 5-year license revocation; admissible in license revocation hearing.

(4) Test Result: No immediate license sanction.

Chemical Testing:

(1) Legal Aspects: Department of Health is authorized to establish administrative rules and regulations.

(2) Blood Test: Withdrawal for police testing must be administered by a physician, registered nurse, licensed and qualified phlebotomist or person licensed in certain clinical laboratory occupations.

(3) Test Result: Upon request, results must be provided to the defendant.

(4) Independent Chemical Test: In addition to any police test, defendants have the right to request and pay for an independent chemical test from a qualified person of their choice. The result

is admissible. The failure or inability to obtain an additional test does not preclude the admissibility of the police test.

IDAHO

Relevant Statute: §§ 18-8004 to 18-8008

Definition of Driving: Driving or actual physical control (in the driver's position of the motor vehicle with the motor running or vehicle moving), while upon a highway, street or bridge, or upon public or private property open to the public.

Drunk Driving Offenses:
(1) BAC of .08 or more (.04 for commercial vehicles). (per se offense)
(2) Under the influence of alcohol, drugs, or other intoxicating substances. (DUI offense)
(3) Driving by a habitual user of, or while under the influence of, a narcotic drug or any other drug, or combination of drugs and alcohol.

Legal Impairment:
(1) For DUI alcohol: No legal standard.
(2) DUI drugs or drugs and alcohol: Incapable of safely driving a motor vehicle.

Penalty Enhancement: 5 years

Penalties:
(1) First offense:
BAC below .20: Maximum 6 months in jail; maximum $1,000 fine; 90 to 150-day license suspension.
BAC .20 or more: 10 days to 1 year in jail; maximum $2,000 fine; additional 1-year license suspension.
(2) Second offense:
BAC below .20: 10 days to 1 year in jail; maximum $2,000 fine; 1-year license suspension.

BAC .20 or more (felony): 30 days to 5 years in prison; maximum $5,000 fine; 1 to 5-year license suspension.

(3) Third or subsequent conviction (felony):
BAC below .20: 30 days to 5 years in prison; maximum $5,000 fine; 1-year license suspension.
BAC .20 or more: 30 days to 5 years in prison; maximum $5,000 fine; 1 to 5-year license suspension.

Implied Consent Laws:

(1) Chemical Tests Allowed: Blood, breath or urine. Officer can request 2 tests if drugs are involved.

(2) Advisement Required: Penalties for test refusal; right to a hearing; right to independent test; no right to counsel prior to testing.

(3) Test Refusal: Immediate license seizure; 180-day or 1-year license suspension.

(4) Test Result: BAC .10 or more: 90-day or 1-year license suspension.

Chemical Testing:

(1) Legal Aspects: Blood, breath or urine test results are admissible without evidence of testing procedure reliability (calibration, certification, or quality control), if performed by a certified person in accordance to approved methods and regulations in a laboratory operated or approved by the Department of Law Enforcement.

(2) Blood Test: Withdrawal for police testing must be administered by a licensed physician, qualified medical technologist, registered nurse, trained phlebotomist, or other medical personnel trained to withdraw blood. A sample must be preserved for testing by the defendant.

(3) Test Result: No statutory provision for disclosure.

(4) Independent Chemical Test: In addition to any police test, defendants have the right to request and pay for an independent chemical test from a qualified person of their choice. The failure or inability to obtain an additional test does not preclude the admissibility of the police test unless the officer denied an additional test.

ILLINOIS

Relevant Statute: 625 § 5/11-501

Definition of Driving: Driving or having actual physical control of any vehicle within the state.

Drunk Driving Offenses:
(1) BAC of .10 or more.
(2) Under the influence of alcohol, any drug, or combination thereof.
(3) Substance in blood resulting from the unlawful use or consumption of cannabis or a controlled substance.

Legal Impairment:
(1) DUI alcohol: No longer possessing clearness of intellect and control normally exhibited.
(2) DUI drugs or combined alcohol and drugs: Incapable of safely driving.

Penalty Enhancement: 5 years

Penalties:
(1) First offense: Maximum 1 year in jail; $500-$1,000 fine; minimum 5 days of community service; license revocation.
(2) Second offense: 48 hours to 1 year in jail or 10 days of community service; $500-$1,000 fine; license revocation.
(3) Third or subsequent offense (aggravated DUI, class 4 felony): 1-3 years in prison; maximum $10,000 fine; license revocation.

Implied Consent Laws:
(1) Chemical Tests Allowed: Blood, breath or urine as selected by officer; PBT.
(2) Advisement Required: Penalties for refusal; license suspension.
(3) Test Refusal: 6-month to 2-year license suspension; no penalty for refusing PBT unless involved in accident resulting in injury or death; admissible in any proceeding arising out of incident.

(4) Test Result: BAC is .10 or more: 3-month to 4-year license suspension.

Chemical Testing:
(1) Legal Aspects: Chemical tests must be performed by a person with a valid permit in accordance to standards approved by the Department of Public Health and Department of State Police.
(2) Blood Test: Withdrawal for police testing must be administered by a licensed physician, registered nurse, trained phlebotomist, certified paramedic, or other qualified person approved by the Department of Public Health.
(3) Test Result: Upon request, results must be provided to the defendant.
(4) Independent Chemical Test: In addition to any police test, defendants have the right to request and pay for an independent chemical test from a qualified person of their choice. The failure or inability to obtain an additional test does not preclude the admissibility of the police test.

INDIANA

Relevant Statute: §§ 9-30-5-1 to 9-30-6-5

Definition of Driving: Operating a vehicle or motorboat within the state, which extends beyond public highways.

Drunk Driving Offenses:
(1) BAC of .10 or more. (per se alcohol offense)
(2) Controlled substance or its metabolite in the person's blood. (per se drug offense)
(3) Under the influence of alcohol, controlled substance, drugs, or any combination thereof. (OWI offense)

Legal Impairment: Impaired condition of thought and action and losing normal control of faculties to such an extent as to endanger others.

Penalty Enhancement: 5 years

Penalties:

(1) First offense (per se alcohol or per se drug offense): Maximum 60 days in jail; maximum $500 fine; 90-day to 2-year license suspension.

(2) First offense (OWI offense): Maximum 1 year in jail; maximum $5,000 fine; 90-day to 2-year license suspension.

(3) Second or subsequent conviction (class D felony): 6 months to 3 years in prison; maximum $10,000 fine; 180-day to 2-year license revocation.

Implied Consent Laws:

(1) Chemical Tests Allowed: Blood, breath, urine or other bodily substance as selected by officer; consent requires compliance with all tests offered; officer can use reasonable force when administering a sample.

(2) Advisement Required: Penalties for refusal.

(3) Test Refusal: 1-year license suspension; admissible in criminal trial.

(4) Test Result: BAC .10 or more: 180-day license suspension.

Chemical Testing:

(1) Legal Aspects: Chemical test result is admissible if performed within 3 hours of driving by a certified operator in accordance with approved methods and procedures; appropriate certification is prima facie evidence that the equipment was inspected, approved, and in proper working order within 180 days of the date of the test.

(2) Blood Test: Withdrawal for police testing must be administered by a licensed physician, or trained person under direction of licensed physician, registered nurse, licensed practical nurse, advanced emergency medical technician, or paramedic.

(3) Test Result: Must be disclosed to law enforcement and prosecuting attorney.

(4) Independent Chemical Test: No statutory provision.

IOWA

Relevant Statute: § 321J

Definition of Driving: Operating a motor vehicle in the state.

Drunk Driving Offenses:
(1) BAC of .10 or more. (per se offense)
(2) Under the influence of an alcoholic beverage, any drug, or combination thereof. (OWI offense)

Legal Impairment: Passions are visibly excited or impaired to any extent.

Penalty Enhancement: 12 years

Penalties:
(1) First offense: 48 hours to 1 year in jail; $1,000-$1,500 fine or maximum 200 hours of community service; 180-day license revocation.
(2) Second offense: 7 days to 2 years in jail; $1,500-$5,000 fine; 1-year license revocation.
(3) Third or subsequent offense (class D felony): 30 days to 5 years in prison; $1,500-$7,500 fine; 6-year license revocation.

Implied Consent Laws:
(1) Chemical Tests Allowed: Blood, breath or urine as selected by peace officer; consent is required for blood test; PBT.
(2) Advisement Required: Penalties for refusal; license suspension.
(3) Test Refusal: 240 to 540-day license suspension; admissible in any civil or criminal proceeding arising out of same incident.
(4) Test Result: BAC .10 or more: 180-day to 1-year license revocation.

Chemical Testing:
(1) Legal Aspects: Admissible chemical tests must be performed by a certified person in accordance with methods and using a device approved by the Commission of Public Safety; result is

not admissible if the BAC is less than .10 after deducting the margin of error inherent in the testing device.

(2) Blood Test: Withdrawal for police testing must be administered by a licensed physician, licensed physician's assistant, medical technologist, or registered nurse using new equipment kept under strict sanitary and sterile conditions.

(3) Test Result: Upon request, results must be provided to the defendant.

(4) Independent Chemical Test: In addition to any police test, defendants have the right to request and pay for an independent chemical test from a qualified person of their choice. The failure or inability to obtain an additional test does not preclude the admissibility of the police test.

KANSAS

Relevant Statute: § 8-1567; §§ 8-1001 to 8-1019

Definition of Driving: Operating or attempting to operate any vehicle within the state.

Drunk Driving Offenses:

(1) BAC of .08 or more within 2 hours of operation (.04 for commercial vehicles).

(2) Under the influence of alcohol, any drug, or combination thereof.

(3) Operating by a person who is a habitual user of a narcotic, hypnotic, somnifacient or stimulating drug.

Legal Impairment: A degree that renders the person incapable of safely driving a vehicle.

Penalty Enhancement: 5 years

Penalties:

(1) First offense: 48 hours to 6 months in jail or 100 hours of public service; $200-$500 fine; minimum 360-day license suspension.

(2) Second offense: 90 days (5-day mandatory minimum) to 1 year in jail; $500-$1,000 fine; minimum 1-year license suspension.

(3) Third or subsequent offense (nonperson felony): 90 days to 1 year in jail; $1,000-$2,500 fine; 1-year license suspension.

Implied Consent Laws:

(1) Chemical Tests Allowed: Blood, breath or urine as selected by police officer; PBT.

(2) Advisement Required: Extensive written and oral advisement.

(3) Test Refusal: Minimum 1-year license suspension; admissible in criminal trial; PBT refusal is traffic infraction.

(4) Test Result: BAC .08 or more: 30-day or 1-year license suspension.

Chemical Testing:

(1) Legal Aspects: Chemical test results are admissible; officer can request urine test if drug use is suspected; chemical samples do not have to be preserved.

(2) Blood Test: Withdrawal for police testing must be administered by a person licensed to practice medicine and surgery or a person under the supervision thereof, registered nurse or licensed practical nurse, qualified medical technician, or phlebotomist.

(3) Test Result: Upon request, results must be made available to defendant.

(4) Independent Chemical Test: In addition to any police test, defendants must be given a reasonable opportunity to arrange and pay for an independent chemical test from a qualified person of their choice. If the officer refuses to permit an alternate test, the police test is inadmissible.

Plea Agreements: A diversion agreement is available; otherwise, a defendant cannot avoid the mandatory drunk driving penalties.

KENTUCKY

Relevant Statute: § 189A

Definition of Driving: Operating or being in physical control of a motor or non-motor vehicle anywhere in the state.

Drunk Driving Offenses:

(1) BAC of .10 or more.

(2) Under the influence of alcohol, impairing substance, or combination thereof.

(3) Operating a non-motor vehicle while under the influence of an intoxicating beverage or impairing substance.

Legal Impairment: No degree of impairment is required.

Penalty Enhancement: 5 years

Penalties:

(1) First offense: 48 hours to 30 days in jail (or 2-30 days of community labor program); \$200-\$500 fine; 90-day license revocation.

(2) Second offense: 7 days to 6 months in jail; 10 days to 6 months community labor; \$350-\$500 fine; 12-month revocation.

(3) Third offense: 30 days to 12 months in jail; 10 days to 12 months community labor; \$500-\$1,000 fine; 24-month license revocation.

(4) Fourth or subsequent offense (class D felony): Minimum 120 days to 5 years in prison; \$1,000-\$10,000 fine; 60-month license revocation.

Implied Consent Laws:

(1) Chemical Tests Allowed: Blood, breath or urine as selected by officer; PBT.

(2) Advisement Required: Penalties for test result or refusal; right to independent test; license suspension. PBT advisement: no right to an attorney, refusal is a traffic infraction, and other tests may be requested.

(3) Test Refusal: 6-month to 5-year license suspension.
(4) Test Result: BAC .10 or more: minimum 90-day license suspension.

Chemical Testing:
(1) Legal Aspects: Admissible chemical test results must be conducted in accordance to regulations established by the Secretary of Justice Cabinet. Test must be performed within a reasonable time after driving incident.
(2) Blood Test: Withdrawal for police testing must be administered by a physician, registered nurse, phlebotomist, or medical technician or technologist.
(3) Test Result: No statutory provision for disclosure.
(4) Independent Chemical Test: In addition to any police test, defendants have the right to request and pay for an independent chemical test from a qualified person of their choice.

Plea Agreements: The prosecutor can reduce drunk driving charges provided the witnesses are unavailable for trial, the scientific evidence is in error, and the reasons are made part of the court record.

LOUISIANA

Relevant Statute: §§ 14:98; 32:414; 32:661 to 32:664B

Definition of Driving: Operating or actual physical control of any motor vehicle, aircraft, watercraft, vessel or other means of conveyance within the state.

Drunk Driving Offenses:
(1) BAC of .10 or more (.04 for minors).
(2) Under the influence of alcoholic beverages or a controlled dangerous substance.

Legal Impairment: Ability to operate a motor vehicle is diminished to the slightest extent.

Penalty Enhancement: 10 years for criminal offense; 5 years for driver's license sanctions

Penalties:

(1) First offense: 10 days to 6 months in jail; $125-$500 fine; 90-day license suspension.

(2) Second offense: 30 days to 6 months in jail; $300-$1,000 fine; 365-day license suspension.

(3) Third offense: 1-5 years in prison; maximum $2,000 fine; 365-day license suspension.

(4) Fourth offense: 10-30 years in prison; maximum $5,000 fine; 365-day license suspension.

Implied Consent Laws:

(1) Chemical Tests Allowed: Blood, breath or urine as selected by officer.

(2) Advisement Required: Miranda rights; penalties for test result and refusal; license suspension.

(3) Test Refusal: Immediate license seizure; 180 to 545-day license suspension; admissible in proceedings arising out of same incident.

(4) Test Result: BAC .10 or more (.04 for minor): 90 to 365-day license suspension.

Chemical Testing:

(1) Legal Aspects: A valid chemical test must be performed by a person with a valid permit in accordance with techniques and methods approved by the Department of Public Safety. Strict compliance with regulations is required.

(2) Blood Test: Withdrawal for police testing must be administered by a physician, registered nurse, qualified technician, or chemist.

(3) Test Result: Upon request, results must be made available to the defendant.

(4) Independent Chemical Test: In addition to any police test, defendants have the right to request and pay for an independent chemical test from a qualified person of their choice. The failure or inability to obtain an additional test does not preclude the admissibility of the police test.

MAINE

Relevant Statute: 29A §§ 2411 to 2528

Definition of Driving: Operating a motor vehicle within the state.

Drunk Driving Offenses:
(1) BAC of .08 or more.
(2) Under the influence of intoxicants.

Legal Impairment: Physical or mental faculties are diminished to the slightest extent.

Penalty Enhancement: 10 years

Penalties: (Test refusal has slightly higher penalties)
(1) First offense: Minimum 48 hours in jail; $400 fine; 90-day license suspension. Mandatory 48 hours in jail for aggravating factors, such as BAC .15 or more, or a test refusal.
(2) Second offense: Minimum 7 days in jail; $600 fine; 18-month license revocation.
(3) Third offense: Minimum 30 days in jail; minimum $1,000 fine; 4-year license revocation.
(4) Fourth or subsequent offense: Minimum 6 months in jail; $2,000 fine; 6-year license revocation.

Implied Consent Laws:
(1) Chemical Tests Allowed: Blood, breath or urine as selected by officer.
(2) Advisement Required: Penalties for test refusal; admissible evidence; considered aggravating factor in sentencing unless the defendant is given an improper advisement.
(3) Test Refusal: 180-day or 1-year license suspension; admissible evidence.
(4) Test Result: No immediate license sanction.

Chemical Testing:

(1) Legal Aspects: Chemical test result is admissible if performed by a certified operator in accordance with approved methods and procedures approved by the Department of Human Services; appropriate certification is prima facie evidence that the test result is accurate.

(2) Blood Test: Withdrawal for police testing must be administered by a licensed physician, registered physician's assistant, registered nurse or person certified by the Department of Human Services.

(3) Test Result: Upon request, result must be provided to the defendant.

(4) Independent Chemical Test: In addition to any police test, defendants have the right to request and pay for an independent chemical test from a qualified person of their choice. The failure or inability to obtain an additional test does not preclude the admissibility of the police test.

MARYLAND

Relevant Statute: Transp. Code §§ 16-205; 21-902; 27-101; C & JP §§ 10-301 to 10-307

Definition of Driving: Driving or attempting to drive any vehicle within the state.

Drunk Driving Offenses:

(1) BAC .10 or more. (DWI offense)

(2) Under the influence of alcohol, drugs, or a combination thereof. (DUI offense)

(3) Under the influence of a controlled dangerous substance.

Legal Impairment:

(1) Alcohol: Ability to operate motor vehicle is significantly diminished.

(2) Drugs: Defendant cannot safely drive a vehicle.

Penalty Enhancement: 3 years

Penalties:

(1) First DUI offense: Maximum 2 months in jail; maximum $500 fine; 45-day license suspension.

(2) Second or subsequent DUI offense: Maximum 1 year in jail; maximum $500 fine; 90-day license suspension or revocation.

(3) First DWI offense: Maximum 1 year in jail; maximum $1,000 fine; 6-month license revocation.

(4) Second DWI offense: Minimum 48 hours in jail or 80 hours of community service to 2 years in prison; $500-$2,000 fine; 1-year license revocation.

(5) Third or subsequent DWI offense: Maximum 3 years in prison; maximum $3,000 fine; 18-month license revocation.

Implied Consent Laws:

(1) Chemical Tests Allowed: Breath; blood if breath test is infeasible; PBT.

(2) Advisement Required: Penalties for test refusal; license suspension.

(3) Test Refusal: 120-day or 1-year license suspension; admissible evidence but creates no inference of guilt.

(4) Test Result: BAC .10 or more: 45 or 90-day license suspension.

Chemical Testing:

(1) Legal Aspects: Chemical tests must be administered by a certified person (not the arresting officer) using approved equipment. A signed certification that approved equipment was used constitutes prima facie evidence and is admissible without such testimony. Defendant can compel the toxicologist to testify regarding the accuracy of the test result.

(2) Blood Test: Withdrawal for police testing must be administered by a legally authorized person using equipment approved by the toxicologist under the Postmortem Examiners Commission.
(3) Test Result: No statutory provision for disclosure.
(4) Independent Chemical Test: In addition to any police test, defendants must be given a reasonable opportunity to arrange and pay for an independent chemical test from a qualified person of their choice. If the officer does not request a test, the defendant may request a test and the officer must allow a chemical test.

MASSACHUSETTS

Relevant Statute: Chptr. 90 §§ 24(1)(a) to 24(1)(f)

Definition of Driving: Operating a motor vehicle upon any way or in a place the public has a right of access, or has access as invitees or licensees.

Drunk Driving Offenses:
(1) BAC of .08 or more.
(2) Under the influence of intoxicating liquor, marijuana, narcotic drugs, depressants, stimulant substances, or glue vapors.

Legal Impairment: Diminished capacity to safely operate a motor vehicle.

Penalty Enhancement: 10 years

Penalties:
(1) First offense: Maximum 2½ years in jail; \$500-\$5,000 fine; 6-month license revocation.
(2) Second offense: 60 days to 2½ years in jail, \$600-\$10,000 fine; 2-year license revocation.
(3) Third offense: 180 days to 2½ years in jail (or 2½-5 years in prison); \$1,000-\$15,000 fine; 8-year license revocation.

(4) Fourth: 2-2½ years in jail (or 2½-5 years in prison); $1,500-$25,000 fine; 10-year license revocation.
(5) Fifth or subsequent offense: Minimum 2½ years in prison; $2,000-$50,000 fine; lifetime license revocation.

Implied Consent Laws:
(1) Chemical Tests Allowed: Blood and breath.
(2) Advisement Required: Penalties for test refusal.
(3) Test Refusal: 120-day to 1-year license revocation; admissible in license revocation hearing.
(4) Test Result: BAC .08 or more: 6-month license revocation.

Chemical Testing:
(1) Legal Aspects: Chemical tests must be performed by a person with a valid permit in accordance with approved methods and regularly certified and maintained equipment that complies with regulations and standards adopted by the Secretary of Public Safety.
(2) Blood Test: Withdrawal for police testing must be administered by a physician, registered nurse, or certified medical technician.
(3) Test Result: Upon request, results must be provided to the defendant.
(4) Independent Chemical Test: In addition to any police test, defendants must be given a reasonable opportunity to arrange and pay for an independent chemical test from a qualified person of their choice.

MICHIGAN

Relevant Statute: § 9.2325

Definition of Driving: Operating a vehicle upon a highway or other place open to the general public or generally accessible to motor vehicles, including an area designated for the parking of vehicles, within the state.

Drunk Driving Offenses:

(1) BAC of .10 or more. (per se offense)

(2) Under the influence of intoxicating liquor, controlled substance, or combination thereof. (OWI offense)

(3) Ability to operate is visibly impaired by the consumption of intoxicating liquor, a controlled substance, or combination thereof. (impaired offense)

Note: It is a criminal offense to authorize or permit a vehicle to be operated by a person in violation of the drunk driving statute punishable with a maximum 90 days in jail and $100-$500 fine.

Legal Impairment:

(1) Intoxicating liquor (OWI offense): Substantially and materially affects ability to drive.

(2) Intoxicating liquor (impaired offense): Less ability than an ordinary careful and prudent driver, which is visible to an ordinary observant person.

Penalty Enhancement: 7 years; 10 years for third or subsequent offenses.

Penalties:

(1) First OWI or per se offense: Maximum 90 days in jail; maximum 45 days of community service; $100-$500 fine; 6-month to 2-year license suspension.

(2) Second OWI or per se offense: 48 hours to 1 year in jail; 10-90 days of community service; $200-$1,000 fine; 6-month to 2-year license revocation.

(3) Third or subsequent OWI or per se offense (class A felony): 1-5 years in prison; $500-$5,000 fine; license revocation.

(4) First impaired offense: Maximum 90 days in jail; maximum 45 days of community service; maximum $300 fine; 90-day to 1-year license suspension.

(5) Second impaired offense: 48 hours to 1 year in jail; 10-90 days of community service; $200-$1,000 fine; 6-month to 2-year license suspension.

(6) Third or subsequent impaired offense: Maximum 1 year in jail; 10-90 days of community service; $200-$1,000 fine; 6-month to 2-year license suspension.

Implied Consent Laws:

(1) Chemical Tests Allowed: Blood, breath or urine; PBT.

(2) Advisement Required: Penalties for test refusal.

(3) Test Refusal: 6-month or 2-year license suspension; admissible in criminal case with statutory instruction; PBT refusal is civil infraction.

(4) Test Result: BAC .10 or more: 6-month to 2-year license suspension.

Chemical Testing:

(1) Legal Aspects: Chemical tests must be performed by a person with a valid permit in accordance with approved methods and regulations adopted by the Department of State Police.

(2) Blood Test: Withdrawal for police testing must be administered by a licensed physician or individual operating under the delegation of a licensed physician.

(3) Test Result: Upon written request, results must be given to the defendant.

(4) Independent Chemical Test: In addition to any police test, defendants must be given a reasonable opportunity to arrange and pay for an independent chemical test from a qualified person of their choice within a reasonable time after detention.

MINNESOTA

Relevant Statute: §§ 169.121 to 169.123

Definition of Driving: Driving, operating, or being in physical control of a motor vehicle within the state or upon the ice of any boundary water of the state.

Drunk Driving Offenses:

(1) BAC of .10 or more (.04 for commercial vehicles) within 2 hours of driving.

(2) Under the influence of alcohol, controlled substance, or combination thereof.

(3) Under the influence of a hazardous substance that substantially impairs driving abilities.

Legal Impairment: Not possessing clearness of intellect and control normally exhibited.

Penalty Enhancement: 5 years; 10 years for third and subsequent offenses.

Penalties:
(1) First offense: Maximum 90 days in jail; maximum $700 fine; minimum 90-day license revocation.
(2) Second offense: Minimum 30 days in jail or maximum 240 hours of community service to maximum 1 year in jail; maximum $3,000 fine; 90-day to 2-year license revocation.
(3) Third or subsequent offense: Minimum 30 days in jail or maximum 240 hours of community service to maximum 1 year in jail; maximum $3,000 fine; 90-day to 2-year license revocation.

Implied Consent Laws:
(1) Chemical Tests Allowed: Blood, breath or urine as selected by peace officer; blood or urine test may be refused unless officer is testing for drugs; PBT.
(2) Advisement Required: Chemical test is required; refusal is a crime; right to contact attorney prior to testing without unreasonable delay.
(3) Test Refusal: 1-year license revocation; admissible in criminal case.
(4) Test Result: BAC .10 or more: 90-day license suspension.

Chemical Testing:
(1) Legal Aspects: No specific statutory provision regarding chemical testing procedures.
(2) Blood Test: Withdrawal for police testing must be administered by a physician, medical technician, physician's trained mobile intensive care paramedic, registered nurse, medical technologist or laboratory assistant.
(3) Test Result: No statutory provision for disclosure.

(4) Independent Chemical Test: In addition to any police test, defendants have the right to an independent chemical test at the place of detention, and at no expense to the state. The failure or inability to obtain an additional test does not preclude the admissibility of the police test. If the officer prevents or denies an additional test, the police test is inadmissible.

MISSISSIPPI

Relevant Statute: §§ 63-11-5 to 63-11-39

Definition of Driving: Driving or operating a vehicle within the state.

Drunk Driving Offenses:
(1) BAC of .10 or more (.08 for minors; .04 for commercial vehicles). (per se offense)
(2) Under the influence of intoxicating liquor, any drug, controlled substance, or any other substance that impairs the ability to operate a motor vehicle. (DUI offense)

Legal Impairment: Slightest degree of impairment.

Penalty Enhancement: 5 years

Penalties:
(1) First offense: Maximum 48 hours in jail; $250-$1000 fine; 90-day to 1-year license suspension.
(2) Second offense: 10 days to 1 year in jail; 10 days to 1 year of community service; $600-$1,500 fine; 2-year license suspension.
(3) Third or subsequent offense (felony): 1-5 years in prison; $2,000-$5,000 fine; 5-year license suspension; vehicle forfeiture.

Implied Consent Laws:
(1) Chemical Tests Allowed: Breath required; may consent to blood or urine test; PBT.

(2) Advisement Required: Penalties for test refusal; right to contact legal or medical assistance.
(3) Test Refusal: Immediate license forfeiture; 90-day or 1-year license suspension; admissible in criminal case.
(4) Test Result: BAC .10 or more: 90-day or 1-year license suspension.

Chemical Testing:
(1) Legal Aspects: Chemical test must be performed by a person with a valid permit in accordance with methods and techniques approved by the State Crime Laboratory and the Commissioner of Public Safety with certification that breath testing equipment is accurate.
(2) Blood Test: Withdrawal for police testing must be administered by a physician, mortician, registered nurse, clinical laboratory technologist or technician, or any other qualified person.
(3) Test Result: Upon written request, results must be provided to the defendant.
(4) Independent Chemical Test: In addition to any police test, defendants have the right to request and pay for an independent chemical test from a qualified person of their choice. The failure or inability to obtain an additional test does not preclude the admissibility of the police test.

Plea Agreements: A drunk driving charge cannot be reduced to a lesser offense.

MISSOURI

Relevant Statute: §§ 577.010 to 577.049

Definition of Driving: Physically operating, driving or being in actual physical control of a motor vehicle in the state.

Drunk Driving Offenses:
(1) BAC of .10 or more. (per se offense)
(2) Intoxicated or drugged condition. (OWI offense)

Legal Impairment: None specified.

Penalty Enhancement: 7 years; 10 years for third or subsequent offenses.

Penalties:

(1) First OWI offense: Maximum 6 months in jail; maximum $500 fine; 30-day license suspension.

(2) First per se offense: Maximum 15 days in jail; maximum $300 fine.

(3) Second offense (per se or OWI): 48 hours to 1 year in jail; maximum $1,000 fine; 5-year license revocation.

(4) Third offense (per se or OWI) (class D felony): Maximum 5 years in prison; maximum $5,000 fine; 10-year license revocation.

Implied Consent Laws:

(1) Chemical Tests Allowed: Blood, breath, urine or saliva; maximum of 2 tests can be given by officer.

(2) Advisement Required: Penalties for refusal; refusal is admissible; 20 minutes to contact attorney.

(3) Test Refusal: 1-year license revocation; admissible in OWI case.

(4) Test Result: No immediate license sanction.

Chemical Testing:

(1) Legal Aspects: A valid chemical test must be performed by licensed medical personnel or a person possessing a valid permit issued by the Division of Health on approved devices pursuant to methods and techniques established by the State Division of Health.

(2) Blood Test: Withdrawal for police testing must be administered by a licensed physician, registered nurse, or trained medical technician at their place of employment using a previously unused, sterile needle and vessel. Strict compliance with accepted medical practices is required, and a nonalcoholic antiseptic must be used when cleaning the skin prior to withdrawal.

(3) Test Result: Upon request, test results must be provided to the defendant.
(4) Independent Chemical Test: In addition to any police test, defendants have the right to request and pay for an independent chemical test from a qualified person of their choice. The failure or inability to obtain an additional test does not preclude the admissibility of the police test.

MONTANA

Relevant Statute: §§ 61-8-401 to 61-8-406; 61-8-714 to 61-8-723; 61-5-205 to 61-5-208

Definition of Driving: DUI alcohol offense: Driving or actual physical control of a vehicle upon the ways of the state open to the public. Other offenses: Driving or actual physical control of a vehicle within the state.

Drunk Driving Offenses:
(1) BAC of .10 or more. (per se offense)
(2) Under the influence of alcohol, dangerous drugs, any other drug, or combination thereof. (DUI offense)

Legal Impairment: Ability to safely operate a motor vehicle is diminished.

Penalty Enhancement: 5 years

Penalties:
(1) First DUI offense: 24 hours to 60 days in jail; $100-$500 fine; 6-month license suspension.
(2) Second DUI offense: 7 days to 6 months in jail; $300-$500 fine; 1-year license revocation.
(3) Third DUI offense: 30 days to 1 year in jail; $500-$1,000 fine; 1-year license revocation.
(4) First per se offense: Maximum 10 days in jail; $100-$500 fine; 6-month license suspension.

(5) Second per se offense: 48 hours to 30 days in jail; $300-$500 fine; 1-year license revocation
(6) Third per se offense: 48 hours to 6 months in jail; $500-$1,000 fine; 1-year license revocation.
(7) Fourth or subsequent per se offense (felony): 6-13 months in jail; 1-4 years probation; $1,000-$10,000 fine; 1-year license revocation; vehicle forfeiture.

Implied Consent Laws:
(1) Chemical Tests Allowed: Blood, breath or urine as selected by officer; PBT.
(2) Advisement Required: Right to refuse PBT; penalties for PBT refusal.
(3) Test Refusal: Immediate license seizure; 6-month or 1-year license suspension; admissible in any proceeding arising out of same incident.
(4) Test Result: BAC .10 or more: 6-month to 1-year license suspension.

Chemical Testing:
(1) Legal Aspects: Chemical test results are admissible if performed by a person with a valid permit in accordance with methods approved by the forensic science division of the Department of Justice in a laboratory approved by the Department of Justice. Valid PBT testing requires officer training and equipment certification.
(2) Blood Test: Withdrawal for police testing must be administered by a physician, registered nurse, or other qualified person under the supervision and direction of a physician or registered nurse.
(3) Test Result: Upon request, results must be provided to the defendant.
(4) Independent Chemical Test: In addition to any police test, defendants have the right to request and pay for an independent chemical test from a qualified person of their choice. The failure or inability to obtain an additional test does not preclude the admissibility of the police test.

NEBRASKA

Relevant Statute: §§ 60-6,196 to 60-6, 211

Definition of Driving: Operating or actual physical control of any motor vehicle within the state.

Drunk Driving Offenses:
(1) BAC of .10 or more. (per se offense)
(2) Under the influence of alcoholic liquor or any drug. (OWI offense)

Legal Impairment: Ability to operate a motor vehicle in a prudent and cautious manner is diminished to any appreciable degree.

Penalty Enhancement: 8 years

Penalties:
(1) First offense: 7-60 days in jail; $200-$500 fine; 6-month license revocation.
(2) Second offense: 7-60 days in jail; $200-$500 fine; 1-year license revocation.
(3) Third or subsequent offense: 7-60 days in jail; $200-$500 fine; 15-year license revocation.

Implied Consent Laws:
(1) Chemical Tests Allowed: Blood, breath or urine as selected by officer; PBT.
(2) Advisement Required: Penalties for PBT and chemical test refusal.
(3) Test Refusal: 1-year license revocation; PBT refusal is class 5 misdemeanor; admissible in criminal case.
(4) Test Result: No immediate license sanction.

Chemical Testing:
(1) Legal Aspects: Chemical test must be performed by a person with a valid permit in accordance with methods and techniques

approved by the Department of Health and Human Services Regulation and Licensure.

(2) Blood Test: Withdrawal for police testing must be administered by a physician, registered nurse, qualified technician, trained person or certified laboratory.

(3) Test Result: Upon request, results must be made available to the defendant.

(4) Independent Chemical Test: In addition to any police test, defendants have the right to request and pay for an independent chemical test from a qualified person of their choice. If the officer refuses an additional test, the police test is inadmissible.

NEVADA

Relevant Statute: §§ 484.379 to 484.393

Definition of Driving: Driving or actual physical control of a vehicle while on a highway or property accessible to the public.

Drunk Driving Offenses:

(1) BAC of .10 or more within 2 hours of driving. (per se offense)

(2) Under the influence of intoxicating liquor, controlled substance or combination thereof, or inhales or otherwise ingests, applies, or uses any chemical, poison or organic solvent, any compound, or combination thereof. (DUI offense)

(3) Driving by a person who is a habitual user of a controlled substance.

Legal Impairment: Habitual user: To an extent that renders the person incapable of safely driving or exercising actual physical control of a vehicle.

Penalty Enhancement: 7 years

Penalties:

(1) First offense: 2 days to 6 months in jail; $200-$1,000 fine; 48 hours of community service; 90-day license suspension.

(2) Second offense: 10 days to 6 months in jail or residential confinement; $500-$1,000 fine; 1-year license suspension.
(3) Third or subsequent offense: 1-6 years in prison; $2,000-$5,000 fine; 3-year license suspension.

Implied Consent Laws:
(1) Chemical Tests Allowed: Blood, breath or urine as selected by officer; blood or urine if officer suspects drug impairment; defendant has right to independent test; PBT.
(2) Advisement Required: Penalties for PBT and chemical test refusal.
(3) Test Refusal: 1 or 3-year license revocation; admissible in criminal and license suspension proceeding; 90-day license revocation for refusing PBT.
(4) Test Result: BAC .10 or more: 90-day license revocation.

Chemical Testing:
(1) Legal Aspects: Chemical test results are admissible if performed by a certified person on an instrument properly calibrated and maintained by the Committee on Testing for Intoxication. The law presumes the device was properly operated. Breath test admissibility requires 2-3 consecutive samples where the BAC results are within .02 or less; otherwise, a blood test is administered.
(2) Blood Test: Withdrawal for police testing must be administered by a physician, physician's assistant, registered nurse, licensed practical nurse, emergency medical technician, or technologist, and the test must be performed on whole blood.
(3) Test Result: Upon request, results must be made available to the defendant.
(4) Independent Chemical Test: In addition to any police test, defendants must be given a reasonable opportunity to arrange and pay for an independent chemical test from a qualified person of their choice. The failure or inability to obtain an additional test does not preclude the admissibility of the police test or the test refusal.

Plea Agreements: A drunk driving or per se charge can be reduced to a lesser offense if the prosecutor knows or it is obvious that the charge is not supported by probable cause or cannot be proven at trial.

NEW HAMPSHIRE

Relevant Statute: § 265:82 to 265:93

Definition of Driving: Driving or attempting to drive a vehicle upon any way.

Drunk Driving Offenses:

(1) BAC of .08 or more (.02 for minors). (per se offense)

(2) Under the influence of intoxicating liquor, controlled drugs, or combination thereof. (DWI offense)

Legal Impairment: Any degree of impairment.

Penalty Enhancement: 7 years

Penalties:

(1) First offense: Minimum $350 fine; 6-month to 2-year license revocation.

(2) Second or subsequent offense: 10 days to 1 year in jail; minimum $500 fine; minimum 3-year license revocation.

(3) Third or subsequent offense: 30 days to 1 year in jail; 28-day treatment program; minimum $500 fine; indefinite license revocation.

Implied Consent Laws:

(1) Chemical Tests Allowed: Blood, breath or urine as selected by officer; PBT.

(2) Advisement Required: Penalties for test refusal; right to independent chemical test.

(3) Test Refusal: 180-day to 2-year license revocation: admissible in any subsequent proceeding; no penalty for refusing PBT.

(4) Test Result: BAC .08 or more: 6-month to 2-year license revocation.

Chemical Testing:

(1) Legal Aspects: Valid and admissible chemical tests must be performed by a certified person in accordance to methods of the Department of Health and Human Services. Blood and breath test samples must be preserved and made available to the defendant.

(2) Blood Test: Withdrawal for police testing must be administered by a physician, registered nurse, certified physician's assistant, or qualified medical technician or medical technologist.

(3) Test Result: Must be given to defendant promptly.

(4) Independent Chemical Test: In addition to any police test, defendants have the right to request and pay for an independent chemical test from a qualified person of their choice. The failure or inability to obtain an additional test does not preclude the admissibility of the police test. The defendant is not entitled to release from custody to obtain a test.

Plea Agreements: If the prosecutor files a written report with the attorney general, a DWI or per se offense can be reduced to a lesser charge but only under limited circumstances.

NEW JERSEY

Relevant Statute: § 39-4-50

Definition of Driving: Operating, or permitting another person to operate a motor vehicle.

Drunk Driving Offenses:

(1) BAC of .10 or more.

(2) Under the influence of intoxicating liquor, narcotic, hallucinogenic or habit-producing drugs.

(3) Knowingly permitting your vehicle to be used by a person who will be committing a drunk driving offense.

Legal Impairment: Physical and mental faculties are materially affected making it unsafe to operate a motor vehicle.

Penalty Enhancement: 10 years

Penalties:

(1) First offense: Maximum 30 days in jail; \$250-\$400 fine; 6-month to 1-year license suspension; 12-48 hours of alcohol education.

(2) Second offense: 48 hours to 90 days in jail; 30 days of community service; \$500-\$1,000 fine; 2-year license suspension.

(3) Third or subsequent offense: Minimum 180 days in jail; \$1,000 fine; 10-year license forfeiture.

Implied Consent Laws:

(1) Chemical Tests Allowed: Breath is permitted.

(2) Advisement Required: Penalties for refusal; right to chemical test results; right to independent chemical test.

(3) Test Refusal: 6-month or 10-year license revocation; \$250-\$500 fine; refusal is admissible.

(4) Test Result: No immediate license sanction.

Chemical Testing:

(1) Legal Aspects: A valid breath test must be performed by a certified individual in accordance with methods approved by the attorney general.

(2) Blood Test: No statutory provision authorizing specific individuals to perform the test.

(3) Test Result: Test results must be given to the defendant.

(4) Independent Chemical Test: In addition to any police test, defendants have the right to request an independent chemical test from a qualified person of their choice.

Plea Agreements: If the drunk driving incident causes bodily injury to others, the victim is allowed to consult with the prosecutor prior to dismissal of the charges or filing a proposed plea agreement with the court; however, this does not limit the prosecutor's authority or discretion when the plea agreement is deemed appropriate.

NEW MEXICO

Relevant Statute: §§ 66-8-102 to 66-8-110; also 31-12-7

Definition of Driving: Driving any vehicle within the state.

Drunk Driving Offenses:
(1) BAC of .08 or more. (per se offense)
(2) Under the influence of intoxicating liquor or any drug. (DWI liquor or DWI drug)

Legal Impairment:
(1) DWI liquor: Slightest reduction of mental or physical abilities and affecting the exercise of clear judgment and a steady hand necessary to safely operate a motor vehicle.
(2) DWI drug: Incapable of safely driving a vehicle.

Penalty Enhancement: 5 years

Penalties:
(1) First offense: Maximum 90 days in jail; minimum 48 hours of community service; maximum $500 fine; 90-day license revocation.
(2) Second offense: 72 hours to 364 days in jail; $500-$1,000 fine; 48 hours of community service; 1-year license revocation.
(3) Third offense: 30-364 days in jail; $750-$1,000 fine; 5-year license revocation.
(4) Fourth or subsequent offense (4th degree felony): 6-18 months in jail; maximum $5,000 fine; 5-year license revocation.

Implied Consent Laws:
(1) Chemical Tests Allowed: Blood or breath as selected by officer.
(2) Advisement Required: Right to independent chemical test.
(3) Test Refusal: 1-year license suspension; may be excluded from evidence as irrelevant.
(4) Test Result: 90-day to 5-year license revocation; admissible in any proceeding arising out of same incident.

Chemical Testing:

(1) Legal Aspects: Chemical test results are admissible when using equipment approved by the Scientific Laboratory Division of the Department of Health Service.

(2) Blood Test: Withdrawal for police testing must be administered by a physician licensed professional or practical nurse, or laboratory technician or technologist employed by a hospital or physician.

(3) Test Result: Must be made available to the defendant.

(4) Independent Chemical Test: In addition to any police test, defendants have the right to request an independent chemical test at state expense from a qualified person of their choice.

Plea Agreements: If the BAC was .08 or more, as reported by the police test, a DWI or per se charge cannot be reduced to a lesser offense.

NEW YORK

Relevant Statute: Veh. & Traffic Law §§ 1192 to 1195

Definition of Driving: Operating a motor vehicle on a public highway, private road open to motor vehicle traffic, or a parking lot.

Drunk Driving Offenses: § 1192

(1) BAC of .10 or more (.04 for commercial vehicles; .02 for minors). (per se offense)

(2) Intoxicated. (DWI offense)

(3) Ability impaired by the consumption of alcohol. (DWAI alcohol offense)

(4) Ability impaired by use of a drug. (DWAI drug offense)

Legal Impairment:

(1) DWI offense: Incapable of utilizing the physical or mental abilities necessary to safely operate a vehicle.

(2) DWAI alcohol offense: Physical and mental abilities necessary to safely operate a vehicle are diminished to any extent.

Penalty Enhancement: 5 and 10 years

Penalties:

(1) First DWAI: Maximum 15 days in jail; $300-$500 fine; 90-day license suspension.

(2) DWAI with prior § 1192 conviction within 5 years: Maximum 30 days in jail; $500-$750 fine; 6-month license revocation.

(3) DWAI with 2 or more § 1192 convictions within 10 years: Maximum 180 days in jail; $750-$1,500 fine; 6-month license revocation.

(4) First DWI, per se, or DWAI drug offense: Maximum 1 year in jail; $500-$1,000 fine; 6-month license revocation.

(5) Second DWI, per se, or DWAI drug offense within 10 years (class E felony): Maximum 4 years in prison; $1,000-$5,000 fine; 1-year license revocation.

(6) Third DWI, per se, or DWAI drug offense within 10 years (class D felony): Maximum 4 years in prison; $2,000-$10,000 fine; 1-year license revocation.

Implied Consent Laws:

(1) Chemical Tests Allowed: Blood, breath, urine or saliva as selected by officer; PBT.

(2) Advisement Required: Penalties for test refusal.

(3) Test Refusal: 6-month or 1-year license revocation; $300-$750 civil penalty; admissible with proper advisement.

(4) Test Result: No immediate license sanction.

Chemical Testing: (For chemical tests within 2 hours of driving)

(1) Legal Aspects: Chemical test is presumed valid if performed by person with a Department of Health permit in accordance with administrative rules and regulations.

(2) Blood Test: Withdrawal for police testing must be administered by a physician, registered professional nurse, registered physician's assistant, or certain specified technicians acting under the supervision and direction of a physician.

(3) Test Result: No statutory provision for disclosure.

(4) Independent Chemical Test: In addition to any police test, defendants have the right to request an independent chemical test from a qualified person of their choice.

Plea Agreements: If the district attorney makes a court record that the original charge was not appropriate, a DWI, per se, or DWAI drug charge can be reduced to a DWAI alcohol charge; however, no reduction is allowed if the drunk driving incident resulted in serious personal injury or death to another person.

NORTH CAROLINA

Relevant Statute: §§ 20-138 to 20-179

Definition of Driving: Driving any vehicle (except a horse, bicycle or lawn mower) upon a highway, street, or public vehicular area within the state.

Drunk Driving Offenses:
(1) BAC of .08 or more.
(2) Under the influence of an impairing substance.

Legal Impairment: Mental or bodily faculties are diminished to any appreciable degree.

Penalty Enhancement: Based on numerous aggravating or mitigating factors. Consult an attorney.

Penalties: Based on numerous aggravating or mitigating factors; order approximates first offense through subsequent drunk driving violations.
(1) Level Five Punishment: 24 hours to 60 days in jail; community service or 30-day driving forfeiture; maximum $100 fine.
(2) Level Four Punishment: 48 hours to 120 days in jail; community service or 60-day driving forfeiture; maximum $250 fine.
(3) Level Three Punishment: 72 hours to 6 months in jail; community service or 90-day driving forfeiture; maximum $500 fine.
(4) Level Two Punishment: 7 days to 12 months in jail; maximum $1,000 fine; maximum 4-year license suspension.
(5) Level One Punishment: 14 days to 24 months in jail; maximum $2,000 fine; maximum 4-year license suspension.

Implied Consent Laws:

(1) Chemical Tests Allowed: Breath or blood as selected by officer; PBT.

(2) Advisement Required: Right to refuse test; penalties for test result or refusal; right to independent test; right to consult attorney.

(3) Test Refusal: 12-month license revocation; admissible in criminal case.

(4) Test Result: BAC .08 or more: Minimum 10-day license suspension.

Chemical Testing:

(1) Legal Aspects: Valid chemical tests must be performed by a qualified person with a permit in accordance with state law and pursuant to methods approved by the Commission for Health Services.

(2) Blood Test: Withdrawal for police testing must be administered by a physician, registered nurse, or other qualified person.

(3) Test Result: No statutory provision for disclosure.

(4) Independent Chemical Test: In addition to any police test, defendants must be given a reasonable opportunity, with the officer's assistance, to arrange an independent chemical test from a qualified person of their choice. If the officer does not advise of this right, or fails to permit and assist the defendant in obtaining a test, the police test is inadmissible.

Plea Agreements: The prosecutor must provide a detailed factual explanation in the court record whenever drunk driving charges are voluntarily dismissed or reduced.

NORTH DAKOTA

Relevant Statute: §§ 39-08-01; 39-20-01 to 39-20-07

Definition of Driving: Driving, or actual physical control, of any vehicle on a highway, or upon a public or private area to which the public has a right of access for vehicular use in the state.

Drunk Driving Offenses:
(1) BAC of .10 or more.
(2) Under the influence of intoxicating liquor, any drug or substance, or combination thereof.

Legal Impairment:
(1) DUI intoxicating liquor: Not possessing the clearness of intellect and control one would otherwise possess.
(2) DUI drug offenses: A degree which renders the person incapable of safely driving.

Penalty Enhancement: 5 years; 7 years for fourth or subsequent offenses.

Penalties:
(1) First offense: Maximum 30 days in jail; $250-$500 fine; 90-day license suspension; vehicle impoundment.
(2) Second offense: 4-30 days in jail or 10 days community service; minimum $500 fine; 365-day license suspension; vehicle impoundment.
(3) Third offense: 60 days to 1 year in jail; $1,000 fine; 2-year license suspension; vehicle seizure.
(4) Fourth offense: 180 days to 1 year in jail; $1,000 fine; 2-year license suspension; vehicle seizure.
(5) Fifth or subsequent offense (class C felony): 180 days to 1 year in jail; $1,000 fine; 2-year license suspension; vehicle seizure.

Implied Consent Laws:
(1) Chemical Tests Allowed: Blood, breath, urine or saliva as selected by officer; PBT.
(2) Advisement Required: Penalties for PBT and chemical test refusal.
(3) Test Refusal: 1 to 3-year license suspension; admissible in any proceeding arising out of same incident; PBT refusal is a test refusal unless submitting to a chemical test.
(4) Test Result: BAC .10 or more: 90-day to 2-year license suspension.

Chemical Testing:

(1) Legal Aspects: Chemical tests are prima facie evidence of accurate BAC levels and admissible if the test is performed by a certified person in accordance with methods and using devices approved by the State Toxicologist.

(2) Blood Tests: Withdrawals for police testing must be administered by a physician, or a qualified technician, chemist, or registered nurse.

(3) Test Result: Must be made available to the defendant.

(4) Independent Chemical Test: In addition to any police test, defendants have the right to request and pay for an independent chemical test from a qualified person of their choice. The failure or inability to obtain an additional test does not preclude the admissibility of the police test.

OHIO

Relevant Statute: §§ 4511; 4507.16

Definition of Driving: Operating any vehicle, streetcar or trackless trolley within the state.

Drunk Driving Offenses:

(1) BAC of .10 or more.

(2) Under the influence of alcohol, drug of abuse, or combination thereof.

Legal Impairment: Lacking clearness of intellect and self-control that one would otherwise possess.

Penalty Enhancement: 5 years

Penalties:

(1) First offense: 3 days to 6 months in jail; $200-$1,000 fine; 90-day to 1-year license suspension.

(2) Second offense: 10 days to 6 months in jail; $300-$1,500 fine; 1 to 2-year license suspension; 90 days impoundment.

(3) Third offense: 30 days to 1 year in jail; $500-$2,500 fine; 2 to 3-year license suspension; 180 days impoundment.
(4) Fourth or subsequent offense: 60 days to 1 year in jail; $750-$10,000 fine; 2 to 5-year license suspension; vehicle forfeiture.

Implied Consent Laws:
(1) Chemical Tests Allowed: Blood, breath or urine as selected by officer.
(2) Advisement Required: Penalty for test result and refusal.
(3) Test Refusal: Immediate license seizure; 1 to 5-year license suspension; admissible in evidence.
(4) Test Result: BAC .10 or more: 90-day to 1-year license suspension.

Chemical Testing:
(1) Legal Aspects: Chemical test must be performed by a person possessing a valid permit in accordance with methods approved by the Director of Health and taken within 2 hours of driving.
(2) Blood Test: Withdrawal for police testing must be administered by a physician, registered nurse, or a qualified technician or chemist.
(3) Test Result: Upon request, results must be made available to the defendant.
(4) Independent Chemical Test: In addition to any police test, defendants have the right to request and pay for an independent chemical test from a qualified person of their choice. The failure or inability to obtain an additional test does not preclude the admissibility of the police test.

OKLAHOMA

Relevant Statute: 47 §§ 751 to 761; 47 § 11-902

Definition of Driving: Driving, operating, or actual physical control of a motor vehicle upon the public roads, highways, streets, turnpikes, or other places within the state.

Drunk Driving Offenses:

(1) BAC of .10 or more within 2 hours after the arrest. (per se offense)

(2) Under the influence of alcohol, any other intoxicating substance, or combination thereof. (DUI offense)

Legal Impairment:

(1) DUI alcohol offense: Ability to operate a motor vehicle in a prudent and cautious manner is reduced to any appreciable degree.

(2) DUI drug offense: Incapable of safely driving or operating a motor vehicle.

(3) Impaired driving offense: Ability to operate vehicle is impaired by consumption of alcohol.

Penalty Enhancement: 10 years

Penalties:

(1) Impaired driving offense: Maximum 6 months in jail; $100-$500 fine; 30-day to 12-month license suspension.

(2) First DUI or per se offense: 10 days to 1 year in jail; maximum $1,000 fine; 90-day license revocation.

(3) Second DUI or per se offense (felony): 1-5 years in prison; maximum $2,500 fine; 1-year license revocation.

(4) Third or subsequent DUI or per se offense (felony): 1-10 years in prison; maximum $5,000 fine; 1-year license revocation.

Implied Consent Laws:

(1) Chemical Tests Allowed: Blood, breath, urine or saliva as selected by officer. Defendant has the right to an additional chemical test.

(2) Advisement Required: None.

(3) Test Refusal: 180-day license suspension; admissible in criminal case.

(4) Test Result: BAC .10 or more: 90-day license suspension.

Chemical Testing:

(1) Legal Aspects: Valid and admissible chemical tests must be performed by a qualified and authorized person in accordance

with the rules and regulations of the Board of Tests for Alcohol and Drug Influence. Test samples must be preserved for 60 days for independent testing by the defendant.

(2) Blood Test: Withdrawal for police testing must be administered by a licensed medical doctor, osteopathic or licensed chiropractic physician, registered nurse, licensed practical nurse, certified physician's assistant, or other authorized persons.

(3) Test Result: A written result must be given to the defendant or their attorney.

(4) Independent Chemical Test: In addition to any police test, defendants have the right to request and pay for an independent chemical test from a qualified person of their choice. The failure or inability to obtain an additional test does not preclude the admissibility of other evidence of intoxication.

OREGON

Relevant Statute: §§ 813.010 to 813.300; 161.615 to 161.635

Definition of Driving: Driving a vehicle upon any premise open to the public or highway in the state.

Drunk Driving Offenses:

(1) BAC of .08 or more (.04 for commercial vehicles). (per se offense)

(2) Under the influence of intoxicating liquor, controlled substance, or combination thereof. (DUI offense)

Legal Impairment: Mental and physical faculties are diminished to some perceptible degree.

Penalty Enhancement: None.

Penalties:

Any offense (class A misdemeanor): 48 hours to 1 year in jail (or treatment center) or community service; maximum $2,500 fine; $220 court fee; 1 to 3-year license suspension; diversion program for first offenders.

Implied Consent Laws:

(1) Chemical Tests Allowed: Blood or breath; field sobriety tests.

(2) Advisement Required: Rights and consequences of test result and refusal; driver's license suspension periods and right to a hearing; right to independent test.

(3) Test Refusal: Immediate license seizure; 1 to 3-year license suspension; chemical and field sobriety test results admissible in any proceeding arising out of same incident.

(4) Test Result: BAC .08 or more: 90-day to 1-year license suspension.

Chemical Testing:

(1) Legal Aspects: Chemical test must be performed by a qualified person with a valid permit using certified equipment pursuant to methods approved by the Health Division or the Department of State Police.

(2) Blood Test: Withdrawal for police testing must be administered by a licensed physician or a person acting under the direction or control of a licensed physician.

(3) Test Result: Written results must be given to the defendant.

(4) Independent Chemical Test: In addition to any police test, defendants have the right to request and pay for an independent chemical test from a qualified person of their choice. The failure or inability to obtain an additional test does not preclude the admissibility of the police test.

Plea Agreements: A DUI offense cannot be reduced to any other charge.

PENNSYLVANIA

Relevant Statute: 75 Pa. CS §§ 1547; 3731; also 18 Pa. CS §§ 1101 to 1104

Definition of Driving: Driving, operating, or actual physical control of the movement of any vehicle.

Drunk Driving Offenses:
(1) BAC of .10 or more within 3 hours of driving. (per se offense)
(2) Under the influence of alcohol, a controlled substance, or combination thereof. (DUI offense)

Legal Impairment: To a degree which renders the person incapable of safe driving.

Penalty Enhancement: 7 years

Penalties:
(1) First offense: 48 hours to 2 years in jail; $300-$5,000 fine; 1 to 5-year license suspension.
(2) Second offense: 30 days to 2 years in jail; $300-$5,000 fine; 1 to 5-year license suspension.
(3) Third offense: 90 days to 5 years in jail; $300-$10,000 fine; 1 to 5-year license suspension.
(4) Fourth offense: 1-5 years in jail; $300-$10,000 fine; 1 to 5-year license suspension.

Implied Consent Laws:
(1) Chemical Tests Allowed: Blood, breath or urine as selected by the officer; PBT.
(2) Advisement Required: Penalties for test refusal.
(3) Test Refusal: 1-year license suspension; admissible in criminal proceeding but refusal creates no presumption of intoxication.
(4) Test Result: No immediate license sanction.

Chemical Testing:
(1) Legal Aspects: Breath test results are admissible and presumed accurate if performed by a certified person on a properly calibrated and approved device in accordance with prescribed procedures.
(2) Blood Test: Blood or urine tests must be administered by an authorized person in a licensed and approved laboratory using prescribed procedures and equipment.

(3) Test Result: Upon request, results must be made available to the defendant.

(4) Independent Chemical Test: In addition to any police test, defendants have the right to request and pay for an independent chemical test from a qualified person of their choice. The test results are admissible evidence.

RHODE ISLAND

Relevant Statute: §§ 31-27-2 to 31-27-3

Definition of Driving: Operating or otherwise driving any vehicle in the state.

Drunk Driving Offenses:

(1) BAC .10 or more. (per se offense)

(2) Under the influence of any intoxicating liquor, drugs, toluene, or any controlled substance, or combination thereof. (DUI offense)

(3) Blood presence of any controlled substance. (per se drug offense)

(4) BAC .04 to .10: Minors 18-21 years old. (impaired driving offense)

Legal Impairment: Incapable of safely operating a vehicle.

Penalty Enhancement: 5 years

Penalties:

(1) First DUI or per se offense: Maximum 1 year in jail; $100-$300 fine; approximately $800 in various assessment fees; 10-60 hours of community service; 3 to 6-month license suspension.

(2) Second DUI or per se offense: 10 days to 1 year in jail; $400 fine; approximately $800 in various assessment fees; 1 to 2-year license suspension.

(3) Third or subsequent DUI or per se offense: 6 months to 1 year in jail; $400 fine; approximately $800 in various assessment fees; 2 to 3-year license suspension; vehicle forfeiture.
(4) First impaired driving offense: Maximum $250 fine; maximum 30 hours of community service; 1 to 3-month license suspension.
(5) Second or subsequent impaired driving offense: Maximum $250 fine; $300 highway assessment fine; maximum 60 hours of community service; 3 to 6-month license suspension.

Implied Consent Laws:
(1) Chemical Tests Allowed: Blood, breath or urine; PBT; maximum of 2 tests allowed by police.
(2) Advisement Required: Penalties for test refusal; right to independent test.
(3) Test Refusal: 3-month to 3-year license suspension; admissible in DUI case if defendant testifies; PBT refusal is traffic infraction.
(4) Test Result: No immediate license sanction.

Chemical Testing:
(1) Legal Aspects: A chemical test is admissible if the defendant consented to the test after a proper advisement, and the test was performed by a certified operator in accordance with methods prescribed by the Department of Health and using approved equipment that was tested for accuracy by a qualified person.
(2) Blood Test: Withdrawal for police testing must be administered by a physician, registered nurse, or certified medical technician.
(3) Test Result: Must be mailed to defendant.
(4) Independent Chemical Test: In addition to any police test, defendants must be informed of the right and given a reasonable opportunity to arrange and pay for an independent chemical test from a qualified person of their choice. The failure or inability to obtain an additional test does not preclude the admissibility of the police test. Results are inadmissible if officer refuses to allow an independent test.

SOUTH CAROLINA

Relevant Statute: §§ 56-5-2930 to 56-5-2990

Definition of Driving: Driving any vehicle within the state.

Drunk Driving Offenses: Under the influence of intoxicating liquors, narcotic drugs, etc.

Legal Impairment: None specified.

Penalty Enhancement: 10 years

Penalties:
(1) First offense: 48 hours to 30 days in jail or 48 hours of public service or $200 fine; 6-month license suspension.
(2) Second offense: 48 hours to 1 year in jail or 10 days of public service; $2,000-$5,000 fine; 1-year license suspension.
(3) Third offense: 60 days to 3 years in jail; $3,500-$6,000 fine; 2-year license suspension.
(4) Fourth or subsequent offense: 1-5 years in prison; 3-year license suspension (permanent revocation for 5th or subsequent offense).

Implied Consent Laws:
(1) Chemical Tests Allowed: Breath; blood test if breath sample cannot be supplied; urine for drugs.
(2) Advisement Required: Penalties for test refusal; testing is not mandatory; right to independent test.
(3) Test Refusal: 90-day license suspension; admissible in evidence.
(4) Test Result: No immediate license sanction.

Chemical Testing:
(1) Legal Aspects: Breath test must be administered by a trained and certified person (not the arresting officer) in accordance with methods approved by SLED.

(2) Blood Test: Withdrawal of blood (or urine) for police testing must be administered in a licensed medical facility by a properly trained licensed physician, registered nurse, or other trained medical personnel.

(3) Test Result: Defendant must receive written test results prior to its use in evidence.

(4) Independent Chemical Test: In addition to any police test, defendants must be given a reasonable opportunity to arrange and pay for an independent chemical test from a qualified person of their choice. The officer must provide reasonable assistance. The failure or inability to obtain an additional test does not preclude the admissibility of the police test. The defendant's failure to request an additional test is not admissible.

Plea Agreements: None. Victims have the right to be informed of plea agreements.

SOUTH DAKOTA

Relevant Statute: §§ 32-23-1 to 32-23-16; also 22-6-1 to 22-6-2

Definition of Driving: Driving or actual physical control of any vehicle.

Drunk Driving Offenses:

(1) BAC of .10 or more. (per se offense)

(2) Under the influence of an alcoholic beverage, marijuana, any controlled drug or substance, or combination thereof. (DUI offense)

Legal Impairment:

(1) DUI alcoholic beverage: Lacking clearness of intellect and self-control one would otherwise possess.

(2) DUI drugs or combined alcohol and drugs: Incapable of safely driving.

Penalty Enhancement: 5 years

Penalties:
(1) First offense: Maximum 1 year in jail; maximum $1,000 fine; 30-day to 1-year license revocation.
(2) Second offense: 3 days to 1 year in jail, maximum $1,000 fine; minimum 1-year license revocation.
(3) Third offense (class 6 felony): 10 days to 2 years in prison; maximum $2,000 fine; minimum 1-year license revocation.
(4) Fourth or subsequent offense (class 5 felony): 20 days to 5 years in prison; maximum $5,000 fine; minimum 2-year license revocation.

Implied Consent Laws:
(1) Chemical Tests Allowed: Blood, breath or other bodily substance.
(2) Advisement Required: Penalties for test refusal; right to independent test.
(3) Test Refusal: 1-year license revocation (unless guilty plea is entered); admissible in criminal case.
(4) Test Result: No immediate license sanction.

Chemical Testing:
(1) Legal Aspects: A valid breath test must be administered by a person possessing a valid permit in accordance with prescribed methods.
(2) Blood Test: Withdrawal for police testing must be administered by a physician, laboratory technician, registered nurse, physician's assistant, phlebotomist, expanded role licensed practical nurse, medical technician or medical technologist.
(3) Test Result: Upon request, results must be made available to the defendant.
(4) Independent Chemical Test: In addition to any police test, defendants have the right to request and pay for an independent chemical test from a qualified person of their choice.

Plea Agreements: If the prosecuting attorney files written reasons with the clerk of court, a DUI or per se offense may be reduced or dismissed.

TENNESSEE

Relevant Statute: §§ 55-10-401 to 55-10-412

Definition of Driving: Driving or physical control of any motor vehicle on the public roads and highways of the state, or on streets or alleys, or while on the premises of a shopping center, trailer park or apartment house complex, or any other premises that are generally frequented by the public at large.

Drunk Driving Offenses:
(1) BAC .10 or more.
(2) Under the influence of an intoxicant, marijuana, narcotic drug, or drug producing stimulating effects on the central nervous system.

Legal Impairment: Lacks ability to operate a vehicle in an ordinary and prudent manner.

Penalty Enhancement: 10 years

Penalties:
(1) First offense: 48 hours to 11 months and 29 days in jail; \$350-\$1,500 fine; 1-year license suspension.
(2) Second offense: 45 days to 11 months and 29 days in jail; \$600-\$3,500 fine; 2-year license suspension; vehicle forfeiture.
(3) Third or subsequent offense: 120 days to 11 months and 29 days in jail; \$1,100-\$10,000 fine; 3 to 10-year license suspension; vehicle forfeiture.

Implied Consent Laws:
(1) Chemical Tests Allowed: Blood, breath or urine.
(2) Advisement Required: Penalties for refusal.
(3) Test Refusal: 1-year license suspension; admissible evidence.
(4) Test Result: No immediate license sanction.

Chemical Testing:

(1) Legal Aspects: Chemical tests are admissible upon written report by the director of the State Bureau of Investigation certifying test accuracy, provided the operator is available to testify, if subpoenaed, as a witness or by deposition.

(2) Blood Test: Withdrawal for chemical testing must be administered by a physician, registered nurse, licensed practical nurse, licensed paramedic, licensed emergency medical technician, technologist, certified or registered phlebotomist, or a person with an unlimited medical license acting at the direction of a licensed medical examiner or physician.

(3) Test Result: Upon request, results must be made available to the defendant.

(4) Independent Chemical Test: In addition to any police test, defendants have the right to request and pay for an independent chemical test from a qualified person of their choice.

Plea Agreements: Drunk driving charges cannot be reduced or dismissed.

TEXAS

Relevant Statute: Penal Code §§ 12.21 to 12.34; 49.04 to 49.09; Civil Code Art. 67011-5

Definition of Driving: Driving or operating a motor vehicle in a public place.

Drunk Driving Offenses:

(1) BAC of .10 or more.

(2) Intoxicated by alcohol, a controlled substance, drugs, or combination thereof.

Legal Impairment: Lacking the normal use of mental or physical faculties.

Penalty Enhancement: 10 years for criminal; 5 years for administrative.

Penalties:

(1) First offense: 72 hours to 180 days in jail; maximum $2,000 fine; 60-day license suspension.

(2) Second offense: 30 days to 1 year in jail; maximum $2,000 fine; 120 to 180-day license suspension.

(3) Third or subsequent offense (3rd degree felony): 2-10 years in prison; maximum $10,000 fine; 120 to 180-day license suspension.

Implied Consent Laws:

(1) Chemical Tests Allowed: Blood or breath.

(2) Advisement Required: Penalties for refusal; admissible evidence; right to hearing on license suspension.

(3) Test Refusal: 90-day license suspension; admissible in criminal case.

(4) Test Result: No immediate license sanction.

Chemical Testing:

(1) Legal Aspects: A valid breath test must be administered by certified individuals in accordance with rules and procedures prescribed by the Department of Public Safety. Blood tests must be administered in a sanitary place.

(2) Blood Test: Withdrawal for police testing must be administered by a physician, qualified technician (not emergency medical services personnel), chemist, registered professional nurse, or licensed vocational nurse.

(3) Test Result: Upon request, results must be provided to the defendant.

(4) Independent Chemical Test: In addition to any police test, defendants have the right (within 2 hours after the arrest) to request and pay for an independent chemical test from a qualified person of their choice. The failure or inability to obtain an additional test does not preclude the admissibility of the police test.

UTAH

Relevant Statute: § 41-6-44

Definition of Driving: Operating or actual physical control of a vehicle within the state.

Drunk Driving Offenses:
(1) BAC of .08 or more within 2 hours of driving. (per se offense)
(2) Under the influence of alcohol, any drug, or combination thereof. (OWI offense)
(3) Under the influence of a controlled substance or having its metabolite in the person's body.

Legal Impairment: Incapable of safely operating a vehicle.

Penalty Enhancement: 6 years

Penalties:
(1) First offense: 48-240 hours in jail or 24-50 hours of community service; minimum $700 fine; minimum 90-day license suspension.
(2) Second offense: 240-720 hours in jail or minimum 80 hours of community service; minimum $800 fine; 3-year license revocation.
(3) Third offense (class A misdemeanor to 3rd degree felony): 720-2,160 hours in jail or minimum 240 hours of community service; $2,000-$2,500 fine; 10-year license revocation.

Implied Consent Laws:
(1) Chemical Tests Allowed: Blood, breath or urine as selected by officer; failure to consent to all requested tests is a refusal.
(2) Advisement Required: Penalties for test refusal.
(3) Test Refusal: 1-year license revocation; admissible in any proceeding arising out of same incident.
(4) Test Result: BAC .10 or more: 90-day license suspension.

Chemical Testing:

(1) Legal Aspects: Chemical test results are presumed valid if records were made in the regular course of investigation, at the approximate time of the test, and the information is trustworthy; no right to consult with an attorney.

(2) Blood Test: Withdrawal for police testing must be administered by a physician, registered nurse, practical nurse, or authorized persons.

(3) Test Result: Upon request, results must be made available to the defendant.

(4) Independent Chemical Test: In addition to any police test, defendants have the right to request and pay for an independent chemical test from a qualified person of their choice. The failure or inability to obtain an additional test does not preclude the admissibility of the police test.

Plea Agreements: A OWI or per se charge may be reduced to reckless driving, but the prosecutor must provide a factual basis for the plea in the record and state whether the defendant consumed alcohol or drugs in connection with the offense; if so, the reckless driving offense counts as a drunk driving offense for purposes of the penalty enhancement statute.

VERMONT

Relevant Statute: Title 23 §§ 1201 to 1210

Definition of Driving: Operating, attempting to operate, or actual physical control of any vehicle on a highway.

Drunk Driving Offenses:

(1) BAC of .08 or more. (per se offense)

(2) Under the influence of intoxicating liquor, any other drug, or combination thereof. (OWI offense)

Legal Impairment:
(1) OWI alcohol offense: No longer having full control over the faculties of the mind.
(2) OWI drugs offense: Incapable of safely driving.

Penalty Enhancement: 5 years; 15 years for third and subsequent offenses.

Penalties:
(1) First offense: Maximum 2 years in jail; maximum $750 fine; 90-day license suspension.
(2) Second offense: 48 hours to 2 years in jail; maximum $1,500 fine; 18-month license suspension.
(3) Third or subsequent offense: Maximum 5 years in prison; maximum $2,500; lifetime license revocation.

Implied Consent Laws:
(1) Chemical Tests Allowed: Breath; blood for drugs and when breath test is infeasible; right to consult with an attorney within 30 minutes; PBT.
(2) Advisement Required: Penalties for test result and refusal; right to consult with an attorney; right to have 2 breath tests performed; refusal is admissible.
(3) Test Refusal: 6-month to lifetime license revocation; admissible in criminal case.
(4) Test Result: BAC .08 or more: 90-day license suspension.

Chemical Testing:
(1) Legal Aspects: It is prima facie evidence of a valid chemical test if performed by a certified person in accordance with the rules and regulations of the Department of Health. Blood samples must be preserved for at least 45 days so the defendant can perform an independent analysis, which is valid if performed in accordance with approved methods and procedures.
(2) Blood Test: Withdrawal for police testing must be administered by a physician, licensed nurse, medical technician, physician's assistant, medical technologist, or laboratory assistant.
(3) Test Result: No disclosure requirement.

(4) Independent Chemical Test: In addition to any police test, defendants have the right to request and pay for an independent chemical test from a qualified person of their choice. The failure or inability to obtain an additional test does not preclude the admissibility of the police test unless the police prevented or denied the additional test. Defendant can also have police sample independently tested or can consent to a second breath test.

VIRGINIA

Relevant Statute: §§ 18.2-266 to 18.2.271

Definition of Driving: Driving, operating, or in actual physical control of a motor vehicle, engine, train or moped upon a public highway.

Drunk Driving Offenses:
(1) BAC of .08 or more. (per se offense)
(2) Under the influence of alcohol, narcotic drug or self-administered intoxicant or drug, or combination thereof. (DUI offense)

Legal Impairment:
(1) DUI alcohol: None specified.
(2) DUI drugs or combined alcohol and drugs: A degree which impairs the person's ability to safely drive or operate a motor vehicle.

Penalty Enhancement: 5 and 10 years

Penalties:
(1) First offense: Maximum 12 months in jail; maximum $1,000 fine, 6-month license suspension.
(2) Second offense (within 5 years): 1 month to 1 year in jail (48 hours mandatory); $200-$2,500 fine; 3-year license revocation.
(3) Second offense (within 10 years): Maximum 1 year in jail; $200-$2,500 fine: 3-year license revocation.

(4) Third or subsequent offense (within 5 years): 2 months to 1 year in jail (30 days mandatory); $500-$2,500 fine; indefinite license revocation.

(5) Third or subsequent offense (within 10 years): 2 months to 1 year in jail (10 days mandatory); $500-$2,500 fine; indefinite license revocation.

Implied Consent Laws:

(1) Chemical Tests Allowed: Breath; blood for drugs or when breath test is infeasible; PBT.

(2) Advisement Required: Right to refuse PBT; penalties for chemical test refusal; right to observe testing procedures and results.

(3) Test Refusal: 6-month or 1-year consecutive license revocation; admissible as rebuttal evidence.

(4) Test Result: BAC .08 or more: Minimum 6-month license suspension.

Chemical Testing:

(1) Legal Aspects: Breath test results are admissible as evidence if administered by a licensed person using equipment tested for accuracy every 6 months and pursuant to methods approved by the Division of Forensic Science.

(2) Blood Test: Withdrawal for police testing must be administered by a physician, registered professional nurse, graduate laboratory technician, or technician or nurse designated by order of a circuit court upon recommendation of a licensed physician using a previously unused, sterile needle and vessel. Substantial compliance with accepted medical practices is required, and a nonalcoholic antiseptic must be used when cleaning the skin prior to withdrawal.

(3) Test Result: Defendant is entitled to observe the test analysis and receive a copy of any results.

(4) Independent Chemical Test: No statutory right.

WASHINGTON

Relevant Statute: §§ 46.61.502 to 46.61.506; 46.20.308

Definition of Driving: Driving or actual physical control of a motor vehicle within the state.

Drunk Driving Offenses:
(1) BAC of .10 or more within 2 hours of driving.
(2) Under the influence or affected by intoxicating liquor, any drug, or combination thereof.

Legal Impairment: Mental or physical faculties affected to the slightest degree.

Penalty Enhancement: 5 years

Penalties:
(1) First offense: 1 day to 1 year in jail; $350-$5,000 fine; 90-day license suspension. If BAC .15 or more or test refusal: 2 days to 1 year in jail; $500-$5,000 fine; 120-day license suspension.
(2) Second offense: 30 days to 1 year in jail; $500-$5,000 fine; 1-year license revocation. If BAC .15 or more or test refusal: 45 days to 1 year in jail; $750-$5,000 fine; 450-day license suspension; vehicle forfeiture.
(3) Third or subsequent offense: 90 days to 1 year in jail; $1,000-$5,000 fine; 2-year license revocation. If BAC .15 or more or test refusal: 120 days to 1 year in jail; $1,500-$5,000 fine; 3-year license suspension; vehicle forfeiture.

Implied Consent Laws:
(1) Chemical Tests Allowed: Breath; blood if breath test is infeasible.
(2) Advisement Required: Right to refuse test; penalties for test result and refusal; right to independent test; refusal is admissible in criminal trial.
(3) Test Refusal: 1 or 2-year license revocation; admissible in criminal trial.

Chemical Testing:

(1) Legal Aspects: Chemical test must be performed by a person with a valid permit in accordance to methods approved by the state toxicologist.

(2) Blood Test: Withdrawal for police testing must be administered by a physician, registered nurse, or qualified technician.

(3) Test Result: Upon request, results must be provided to the defendant.

(4) Independent Chemical Test: In addition to any police test, defendants have the right to request and pay for an independent chemical test from a qualified person of their choice. The failure or inability to obtain an additional test does not preclude the admissibility of the police test unless the police prevented or denied the additional test.

WEST VIRGINIA

Relevant Statute: §§ 17C-5-2 to 17C-5-8

Definition of Driving: Driving a vehicle in the state.

Drunk Driving Offenses:

(1) BAC of .10 or more.

(2) Under the influence of alcohol, a controlled substance, any drug, or combination thereof.

(3) Driving by a person who is a habitual user of narcotic drugs or amphetamines, or any derivative thereof.

(4) Knowingly permitting your vehicle to be driven by a person in violation of the drunk driving laws.

Legal Impairment: None specified.

Penalty Enhancement: None specified.

Penalties:

(1) First offense: 1 day to 6 months in jail; \$100-\$500 fine; 6-month license revocation.

(2) Second offense: 6 months to 1 year in jail; $1,000-$3,000 fine; 10-year license revocation.
(3) Third offense (felony): 1-3 years in prison; $3,000-$5,000 fine; lifetime license revocation.

Implied Consent Laws:
(1) Chemical Tests Allowed: Blood, breath or urine as selected by officer; blood test can be refused for alternate test; PBT.
(2) Advisement Required: Penalties for test refusal.
(3) Test Refusal: 1-year to lifetime license revocation; 15 minutes to change refusal to consent; admissible in criminal trial.
(4) Test Result: BAC .10 or more: 6-month to 10-year license suspension.

Chemical Testing:
(1) Legal Aspects: A valid chemical test must be performed in accordance with methods and procedures approved by the Department of Health, and taken within 2 hours after the arrest or the alleged driving. Blood or urine tests must be performed in a qualified laboratory.
(2) Blood Test: Withdrawal for police testing must be administered by a doctor of medicine or osteopathy, registered nurse, or trained medical technician at their place of employment in strict accordance to accepted medical practices utilizing an unused, sterile needle and vessel, and a nonalcoholic antiseptic when cleansing the skin prior to venipuncture.
(3) Test Result: Upon request, results must be provided to the defendant.
(4) Independent Chemical Test: In addition to any police test, or if no police test is requested, defendants have the right to request and pay for an independent chemical test from a qualified person of their choice within 2 hours of the arrest.

WISCONSIN

Relevant Statute: §§ 346.63 to 346.655; 343.30 to 343.31; 973.05

Definition of Driving: Driving or operating a motor vehicle.

Drunk Driving Offenses:
(1) BAC of .10 or more (.04 for commercial vehicles). (per se offense)
(2) Under the influence of an intoxicant, controlled substance, controlled substance analog, any other drug, or combination thereof. (DUI offense)

Legal Impairment:
(1) DUI alcohol: Ability to operate a motor vehicle is materially affected.
(2) DUI drugs: Incapable of safely driving.

Penalty Enhancement: 5 years for criminal; 5 and 10 years for driver's license suspension.

Penalties:
(1) First offense: $150-$300 fine; 6-month license revocation.
(2) Second offense: 5 days to 6 months in jail; $300-$1,000 fine; 1 to 2-year license revocation.
(3) Third offense: 30 days to 1 year in jail; $600-$2,000 fine; 3-year license revocation; vehicle immobilized or forfeiture.
(4) Fourth or subsequent offense: 60 days to 1 year in jail; $600-$2,000 fine; license revocation per court order; vehicle immobilized or forfeiture.

Implied Consent Laws:
(1) Chemical Tests Allowed: Blood, breath or urine as selected by officer; officer can request multiple tests; PBT.
(2) Advisement Required: Penalties for test result and refusal; right to independent test; license suspension.
(3) Test Refusal: Immediate license seizure; 1 to 3-year license revocation; admissible in evidence.
(4) Test Result: BAC .10 or more: 6-month license suspension.

Chemical Testing:
(1) Legal Aspects: A valid breath test must be performed by a certified person in accordance with techniques and methods

approved by the Department of Transportation using instruments certified for accuracy, and infrared breath tester must follow a testing sequence. A valid blood or urine test must be performed by a person having a valid permit in an approved laboratory that substantially complies with methods approved by the Laboratory of Hygiene.

(2) Blood Test: Withdrawal for police testing must be administered by a physician, registered nurse, medical technologist, physician's assistant or person acting under the direction of a physician.

(3) Test Result: No statutory provision for disclosure.

(4) Independent Chemical Test: In addition to any police test, defendants have the right to request and pay for an independent chemical test from a qualified person of their choice. The failure or inability to obtain an additional test does not preclude the admissibility of the police test.

WYOMING

Relevant Statute: §§ 31-5-233; 31-6-102 to 31-6-105; also 31-7-127; 31-7-128

Definition of Driving: Driving or having actual physical control of any vehicle upon a public street or highway within the state.

Drunk Driving Offenses:

(1) BAC of .10 or more. (per se offense)

(2) Under the influence of alcohol, controlled substance, or combination thereof. (DUI offense)

Legal Impairment: Incapable of safely driving.

Penalty Enhancement: 5 years

Penalties:

(1) First offense: Maximum 6 months in jail; maximum $750 fine; 90-day license suspension.

(2) Second or subsequent offense: 7 days to 6 months in jail; $200-$750 fine; 1 or 3-year license suspension.

Implied Consent Laws:

(1) Chemical Tests Allowed: Blood, breath or urine as selected by officer; defendant has choice of blood or urine test unless officer is testing for drugs.

(2) Advisement Required: Penalties for test refusal; right to independent test; license suspension.

(3) Test Refusal: 6 or 18-month license suspension; admissible in any proceeding arising out of same incident.

(4) Test Result: BAC .10 or more: 90-day license suspension.

Chemical Testing:

(1) Legal Aspects: Chemical test must be performed by a person with a valid permit in accordance to methods approved by the Department of Health.

(2) Blood Test: Withdrawal for police testing must be administered by a physician, registered nurse, qualified clinical or laboratory technician or other person who routinely does venipuncture at the direction of a physician.

(3) Test Result: Upon request, results must be made available to the defendant. Independent chemical test results must be made available to the arresting officer.

(4) Independent Chemical Test: In addition to any police test, defendants have the right to request and pay for an independent chemical test from a qualified person of their choice. The failure or inability to obtain an additional test does not preclude the admissibility of the police test.

Plea Agreements: If the prosecuting attorney determines there is insufficient evidence to sustain the charge, a motion in open court or the filing of a statement is sufficient to reduce or dismiss a DUI or per se offense.

Appendix A

GLOSSARY

advisement, implied consent: when a motorist is arrested for drunk driving, the officer is often required to provide information regarding the legal rights and consequences of refusing or consenting to a chemical test for the purpose of determining blood-alcohol concentration levels.

blood test: chemical test that involves withdrawing venous blood for analysis to determine blood-alcohol concentration.

cannabis: commonly referred to as marijuana, and designated as a narcotic and controlled substance requiring a lawful prescription.

chemical test *see also* independent chemical test

diversion agreement: criminal disposition either before or after adjudication of guilt wherein the defendant must participate in a work or educational program as a condition of probation.

enhancement *see* penalty enhancement

independent chemical test: often a statutory right of motorists to request a separate, non-governmentally administered blood test for determining blood-alcohol concentration; the motorist must request the independent test, which is typically given after successful completion of the chemical test requested by the police officer.

inference: a logical deduction that is presumed or suggested by certain facts, but not absolute or an established truth; a deduction or conclusion reached using common sense and reason based upon established facts.

legal presumption *see also* rebuttable presumption

license suspension: resulting from one or more moving violations, and involves the period of time in which a motorist in not entitled to lawfully drive, though may be eligible for a temporary restricted license.

Miranda rights: fifth amendment constitutional right against self-incrimination, having an attorney present, or receiving a court-appointed attorney. Police officers must advise defendants of these rights at the time of arrest. If a defendant is taken into custody or experiences a significant deprivation of freedoms and no waiver of rights is provided, all subsequent admissions are inadmissible at trial.

PBT *see* preliminary breath test

peace officer: law enforcement personnel statutorily obligated to enforce and preserve the peace with authority to make arrests.

penalty enhancement: typically a statutory authorization for the state to charge persons with an increasingly harsher criminal offense with more severe punishment upon each repeated violation of the same law.

penalty enhancement period: time frame in which a statute authorizes the state to escalate the level of criminal offense and the punishment imposed.

permissive inference: an inference that is allowed under the law, and usually set forth by statute or court rules.

per se offense: statutorily defined offenses that are presumed unlawful without the need for additional evidence to establish guilt and criminal culpability; in the drunk driving context, this usually applies to motorists consenting to a chemical test that indicates a blood-alcohol concentration in excess of the legal limit.

phlebotomist: person authorized to perform blood extraction for transfusion, diagnosis or experiment.

preliminary breath test: initial testing of motorists to determine blood-alcohol concentration using hand-held or squad car mounted devices that measure alcohol content in the breath; in most instances the test result is not admissible in court, though it can be considered as a chemical test refusal for the implied consent statute and is available to the judge and prosecutor as a factor in sentencing.

presumption *see* legal presumption

prima facie: evidence considered legally sufficient to establish a fact or group of facts, and if not rebutted or contradicted, will remain conclusively proven as true.

somnifacient: of or relating to sleep, hypnosis or drowsiness.

suspension *see* license suspension

rebuttable presumption: presumption that may be challenged by other evidence, but if the fact is not rebutted, it is presumed to be true.

refusal *see* test refusal

revocation *see* license suspension

test refusal: when a motorist does not voluntarily consent to allowing a peace officer to obtain a chemical test specimen for the purposes of determining their blood-alcohol concentration.

test result: when a motorist voluntarily consents to allow a peace officer to obtain a chemical test specimen for the purpose of determining their blood-alcohol concentration.

UAC: chemical test of bodily urine to determine blood-alcohol concentration, though more commonly used to detect illegal drug usage.

Appendix B

ABBREVIATIONS

ALJ: administrative law judge

BAC: blood-alcohol concentration

DUI: driving under the influence

DWI: driving while intoxicated

FST: field sobriety test

HGN: horizontal gaze nystagmus

IID: ignition interlock device

NHTSA: National Highway Traffic Safety Administration

OWI: operating while intoxicated

OMVUI: operating a motor vehicle under the influence

PBT: preliminary breath test

TRL: temporary restricted license (often referred to as a work permit)

UAC: urine-alcohol concentration